Do People go to Heaven when they Die?

(The Unbelievable Truth about Life and Death!)

By
The Good Pastor of Uncommon Sense!

Book 120 ◆

(The Cover Photo shows a Coffin with a Dead Man, who did NOT go to Heaven; but, he went to the "Slimmetery," or Slim-me-Tiera, which is commonly called the Cemetery, or Graveyard for Rotting Flesh and Bones, which is Preserved with Formaldehyde and whatever else, as if such a Body might be Used again, during the Future, which is Pure Superstitious Religious Nonsense at its Worst; but, People Believe it.)

Copyright, Dedication and Introduction!

By the Honest Observer and Chief Agitator!

ISBN — 979-8655-9755-83

00-01 [_] This Inspired Book is COPYRIGHTED ADR (After Death and Resurrection) 2020. All Rights are Reserved for the Truth's Sake, whatever it might be, which has yet to be Proven at: "The GREAT Worldwide TELEVISED Court HEARING!" (That Great Meeting of the Most-Intelligent and Well-Educated Minds!) By The Worldwide People's Revolution!® Book 041B, including the Exact Date of the Birth of Jesus Christ, which might Help to Identify the Exact Date of his Death: beCause he was Crucified during a Passover, which fell on a Wednesday, at Sunset, which made Thursday a High Sabbath Day, and Friday, or Venus Day, the Normal Preparation Day for the Regular Sabbath Day on Saturn Day, in Latin: beCause, according to the *Holy Bible,* in *Matthew 12:40,* Jesus was Resurrected 3 Nights and 3 Days after he was Buried at Sunset on Mercury Day, or Wedding Day, called Wednesday, which Debunks the Easter Sunrise Sunday Morning Resurrection Nonsense. In other Words, he Arose from the Dead just after Sunset on Saturn Day, which we Traditionally call Saturday, which is just a Lazy Man's Way of Spelling Saturn Day, as the Romans and Greeks called it: beCause they Named the Days of the Week by the Names of Heavenly Bodies. Monday got its Name from Moon Day, which is Lunas in Spanish, which is derived from Lunar Day in Latin. In other Words, the Days of the Week are derived from Pagan Names, even as Easter is, who was the 12-Breasted Goddess of Ancient Babylon.

Easter was originally the celebration of Ishtar, the Assyrian and Babylonian **goddess** of fertility and sex. Mar 31, 2013

blogs.scientificamerican.com › anthropology-in-practice
Beyond Ishtar: The Tradition of Eggs at Easter - Scientific American

00-02 [_] No Portion of this Unique Book shall be Reproduced by any Means for Sale without Written Permission from: "The Worldwide People's Revolution!" (A Comprehensive Plan for Obtaining Worldwide Law, Order, Obedience, Peace and True Prosperity!) By The Worldwide People's Revolution!® Book 108: beCause our Selected King wants 10% of the Net Profits for the Construction of: "The Great World TEMPLE of PEACE!" (The Glory of Jerusalem

Arises Again in the Great State of Flexible Texas!) By The Worldwide People's Revolution!® Book 017B, which will be the Headquarters for: "The New RIGHTEOUS One-World Government!" (HOW to Establish a Righteous One-World Government without Going to WAR!) By The Worldwide People's Revolution!® Book 056: beCause, there are "101 Good Reasons and Great Advantages for Establishing a Righteous One-World Government!" (Government By the People, Of the People, and For the People!) By The Worldwide People's Revolution!® Book 104, whose Elected Righteous King will be a Christian: beCause of "Provable Truths that True Christians cannot Rightly Deny!" (A Fair Challenge for all Professing "Christians" to Meditate on with Honest Open Minds!) By The Worldwide People's Revolution!® Book 086.

00-03 [_] O Good Pastor of Uncommon Sense, what does the Temple of God have to do with a House of Idols? After all, WE Believers are the Temple of the Living God, just as it is Written in Granite Stones in Saint Peter's Basilica, in Rome, which is the Truth of it. †§‡§§

00-04 [_] I Asked Mr. Google, "Who was Easter?" and those are Bits of Information that anyone can Discover on the Internet, if they Search for them. In other Words, it is no Big Secret that Easter was a Pagan Goddess, who was Adopted by Fake Christians, who did not even know the History of their Goddess, who had no Connection with a Resurrection, even as Insanity Claus has nothing to do with the Birth of Jesus Christ, who was NOT Born during Christmas Day: beCause that was just another Pagan Holiday, which was Transformed into a "Christian" Holy Day for Commercial Reasons: beCause, *"The Love of Money is the Root Cause for almost all Evils,"* as the Apostle Paul was trying to say in *First Timothy 6,* who liked to Overuse the Word, ALL, even as most of the *Unholy Mutilated Bible* often does. For Example, in *the Gospel according to Saint John, Chapter 01,* it Reveals that ALL THINGS were Created by Jesus Christ, including the Trillions of Stars in the Billions of Galaxies: beCause, at the Time of the Translations of the *Scriptures,* those Silly Ignorant People actually Believed that the Earth was at the Center of the entire Universe! †§‡

What does God say about Easter?

John 11:25-26. Jesus **said** to her, "I am the **resurrection** and the life. The one who believes in me will live, even though they die; and whoever lives by believing in me will never die.

www.southernliving.com › easter › easter-bible-verses
Easter Bible Verses To Celebrate Resurrection Day | Southern

Is Easter a God?

But in English-speaking countries, and in Germany, **Easter** takes its name from a pagan goddess from Anglo-Saxon England who was described in a book by the eighth-century English monk Bede. "Eostre was a goddess of spring or renewal and that's why her feast is attached to the vernal equinox," Professor Cusack said. Apr 14, 2017

www.abc.net.au › news › the-origins-of-easter-from-paga...
Origin of Easter: From pagan festivals and Christianity to bunnies ...

What was Easter called before Christianity?

In western **Christianity**, including Roman Catholicism and Protestant denominations, the period **prior to Easter** holds special significance. This period of fasting and penitence is **called** Lent. Apr 9, 2020

www.history.com › topics › holidays › history-of-easter
Easter - Dates, Easter Eggs & Easter Bunny - HISTORY

Easter was originally a celebration of Ishtar, the Babylonian goddess of sex, fertility, war, and religiously-sanctioned prostitutes, right? Wrong. Well, bunnies and eggs can't possibly have anything to do with this most holy festival commemorating Jesus Christ's resurrection from the dead, then. Actually… they do.

00-05 [_] So, was Mr. Google Honest? Is that what God Actually Said (Sed) about Easter? NO! So, I went to the *Blue Letter Bible* on the Internet, in order to Search for Ishtar — Thinking that maybe God had Heard about her, and made some Comment in the *Holy Bible,* only to be Greatly Disappointed by the Lack of Information in the Bible. After all, what are the Chances of an Ancient Babylonian Goddess called Ishtar, not being Heard of in Palestine, which was Conquered by the Babylonians? Indeed, that would be like the American Indians never Hearing about Christ, after being Conquered by Christians! Chances are that Babylonians were Worshipers of Ishtar, even as Christians are Observers of Easter, with Rabbits laying Colored Chocolate Eggs.

Would it surprise you to Learn that Ishtar was the single Most-Hated Pagan Goddess, by Jehovah God? But, WHY?

"I did not die. I did not go to Heaven," Malarky wrote. "I said I went to heaven because I thought it would get me attention. When I made the claims that I did, I had never read the Bible. People have profited from lies, and continue to. They should read the Bible, which is enough. The Bible is the only source of truth. Anything written by man cannot be infallible."

00-06 |_| The Name, MALARKY, quite well sums it all up. He was Full of Malarkey. Even his Confession was also Malarkey: beCause, "The Bible is the only source of truth," is nothing but Malarkey: beCause there are many Sources of Provable Truths, including this Inspired Book, and this very Verse, itself. And then his next Line of Lies is Contradictory — "Anything written by man cannot be infallible." However, every Word of the *Holy Bible* was written by MEN, and not by any God. In Fact, *"Holy Men, Inspired by God, wrote the Scriptures, even as they were Moved by the Holy Spirit,"* according to *Second Peter 1:21,* which is Exactly HOW the Good Pastor of Uncommon Sense will write this Extremely Good Book, which will Reveal many Provable Truths that are not found in the so-called *"Holy Bible,"* which does not even Reveal Exactly what Happens to a Person who Dies. Nevertheless, *"All Scriptures are Inspired by God, and are Profitable for Teaching Good Doctrines, for Reproving Sinners, for Correcting Saints, and for Instructions in the Ways of Righteousness: so that the Man of God might be Thoroughly Furnished with the Correct Tools and Materials for Building his House of Love on the Solid Bedrock of Divine Truths,"* as Saint Paul was trying to Explain to Poor Timothy, in *Second Timothy 3:16,* who could not Afford to Buy any Bottled Water; but, only a little Wine for his Stomach's Sake, and his often Sicknesses from Drinking Bad Water. See: *First Timothy 5:23, King James Version.*

00-07 [_] O Honest Observer and Chief Agitator, if we cannot Trust the *Holy Bible* to get it Riit, who or what can we Trust, seeing that the Jews are the most Notorious Liars on the Earth? †§‡§§

00-08 |_| Well, my Friend, I would say that you can Trust the Holy Spirit, if you Keep your Mind on All that is GOOD, which is God. Therefore, Stop Thinking Evil, and Pray to God for Help. ⌂‡

00-09 [_] O Honest Observer and Chief Agitator, I can Do that well, until I get Horny, and then I cannot help but Think Evil, or at least Masturbate myself, just to keep from going Crazy. †§‡§§

00-10 [_] Well, my Friend, that is Time to Fast and Pray, according to: "The Proper RULES for FASTING!" (The Complete Instruction Manual for True Repentance!) By The Worldwide People's Revolution!® Book 046, which will Relieve you of that Craziness.

FOOTNOTE: If any of the Words are too Small to read with Comfort, please see the 8.5 by 11-inch Colored Edition, which is also less Expensive: beCause of having less Sheets of Paper.

The MENU on the Table of Contents for a Feast of Satisfying Provable Truths!

{HEADNOTE: This Inspired Book contains a few Pictures with Explanations, and about 25,000 Unique Words of Great Encouragement. Therefore, do not allow anyone to get you Discouraged by any Means, whereby you might Commit Suicide: beCause, there is Hope for everyone who Believes in All that is Good, which is God, who is Immortal, who cannot Die, who has the Power, the Glory, and the Keys to the Holy Kingdom of All that is Good. Therefore, have Faith in it.}

{Missing Chapters will be Supplied when they are Needed. Chances are that they will never be Needed: beCause it is now Possible for everyone to go to Heaven, right here on the Good Old Earth! And I will tell you HOW to Accomplish that, without telling any Lies.}

FOOTNOTE: For the Explanations of the Symbols (†§‡§§), see: "Which Church is the Right Church?" (Can all Churches be Correct?) **By** The Good Pastor of Uncommon Sense! Book 119. Moreover, if you do not have a Computer, it is Time to get one: beCause there are Mountains of Good Things to be Learned.

— Chapter 01 —

Where did the Notion of People going to Heaven come from?

01-01 [_] Well, it most likely came from the Reality of the Fact that the Original People came to the Earth from "Heaven," or from the Sky, who came to this Earth in Giant Spaceships, which were Inventions of the Giants, themselves, who were Wise Men of Great Renown, just as the *Holy Bible* Reveals in so many Mutilated *Scriptures,* which are Difficult for most People to Understand: beCause the Lying Conniving Edomites did not Want People to Learn much of anything about those Giants: beCause the Edomites Envied them for their Great Strength and Worldly Wisdom, who Built the Great Pyramids, Stonehenge, the Foundations of Jerusalem, Bashan, and many Places in Central and South America, which have Ancient Origins, which can only be Rightfully Explained by the Fact that they are Works of the GIANTS. ‡

01-02 [_] O Good Pastor of Uncommon Sense, are you saying that Mankind did NOT Evolve from Monkeys nor Apes; but, that the Giants Transported the Black and Brown Races of Peoples to this Earth from other Worlds in the Vast Universe, in Order that those Black and Brown Peoples might be their SLAVES and Servants? Did they also bring almost all of the Animals with them, including the Fishes in the Seas, and everything else? Did they also Create Adam and Eve? What was going on back in those Days, anyway?

01-03 [_] Well, God has Revealed to our Selected King that this Good Earth was in Fact and in Deed, Inhabited by Aliens from other Worlds, who used to be Thot of as being "the Gods," which merely Meant "the Supreme Rulers": beCause they have Governed the Inhabitable Worlds since Ancient Times. In Fact, Jehovah God, who Appeared to Moses in *Exodus 33,* in all of his Naked Glory was a GIANT of a Man, which is HOW he Hid Moses in the Cliff of the Rock, and put his Hand over the Hole to Hide the Eyes of Moses from Seeing his Nakedness, which is a True Story: beCause Jehovah / Yahweh God is in Deed a GIANT, and one of the Greatest of the Giants, who now Livz Inside of Jupiter, along with Trillions of People and Holy Angels, many of whom are also Giants; but, Jehovah God is about 400 feet (122 meters) Tall, and about 100 feet Wide at his Shoulders, with a Chest that is about 60 feet Thick, and a Tally Whacker that is about 110 feet Long from the Base, when it is Erect, with Testicles that are as Big as 70-gallon Barrels! Yes, I Know that it is Difficult for most People to Believe that; but, it is the Truth of it, and your Unbelief will not Change the Facts by even one Degree. However, if you Want to Learn more about him, you will have to Study the Inspired Books of our Selected King: beCause, I am not going to Cast our Selected King's Pearls of Provable Truths in front of the Unbelieving Swines, as Jesus said, who come in all Colors and Kinds, who Doubt the GREATNESS of the GODS. However, I will tell this much, that those Gods have been Creating Endless Worlds for Billions upon Billions of Years, whereby they might be Inhabited with Various Kinds of Peoples: beCause the Gods have yet to Discover the Perfect Kind of People to Multiply the Most; but, they are very Busy Experimenting with all Kinds; and the Better Kinds Inhabit the Insides of the Planets, most of which are Inhabited throughout the entire Universe, including a lot of Moons; but, not all of them. In Fact, those Worlds are somewhat like Hollow Geodes, like Agates, you might say, which have Hot Lava Cores between the Hollow Parts and the Surfaces. For Example, this Good Earth has about 1,000 Miles of Mass that Surrounds the Hollow Part, which is the Size of our Moon: beCause our Moon was Born from the Hollow Earth, through the North Hole, which Opened like the Matrix of the Womb of a Womb-man, when she gave Birth to the Moon; and afterwards, the Matrix Closed up to where it is now, at the North Pole, which has a Smaller Hole at the South Pole, which was Sucked Out when the Moon was Born, Billions of Years Ago, after the Planets were Born from the Sunstar in this Solar System, which is just one of Trillions of Solar Systems in the Vast Universe, each of which have a God to Govern it, even if a few of them are a little Crazy, in our Opinions. For Example, most People in this World of Wonders would say that Jehovah God should Appear to us, right now, in all of his Naked Glory: so that we might See the God whom we are supposed to Worship as our Supreme Ruler. However, he Created White People in his own Image.

01-04 [_] O Good Pastor of Uncommon Sense, are you Kidding us? Are you Teasing our Minds, or what? Why would Jehovah God keep himself Hidden from us for all of these thousands of Years, ever since he Revealed himself to Moses on Mount Sinai? What is the Purpose for Doing that? After all, he should have Known that your Selected King would come along and Reveal it. §

01-05 [_] Well, the Purpose was for Jehovah God to Discover WHO might be Worthy to Govern this World with his Chosen Son, whom we call Jesus Christ, whose Name Means "The Anointed Savior," who was the Beginning of the Creation of White Men in this World of Wonders, who was called Adam, who was Placed in the Garden of Eden, within the Hollow Earth, in a Place that is now called Mount Zion, which is the Holy City of the Great King, who is Jesus Christ, which is Written about in *the Book of the Psalms of King David,* which you can Discover in Chapters 48, 50, and 87, if you care to Look. Of course, no one is going to Force you to Look, nor Force you to Think about it. However, David put a Special Word in the Psalms, which is "SELAH," which Means, STOP and THINK, which very few People Do: beCause they are just Ignorant Fools, who have said in their Hearts: *"There is no God,"* in spite of the Fact that there are Countless Creations to Prove it, and much Evidence to Prove that there were also GIANTS. In Fact, David Slew one of those little Giants with his own Sword, called GOLIATH, who was only about 12 feet Tall, who was one of the Last of the Giants on the Surface of this Good Earth; but, you do not have to Believe it, and Yahweh God could care less whether or not you Believe it: beCause Jehovah God is only Looking for BELIEVERS, and OBEYERS, who will Obey the Commandments of his Chosen Son, who became the Second Adam, as the Apostle Paul was Attempting to Explain in *First Corinthians 15,* which was all Written to WEED OUT the Unbelievers, even as our Selected King has Written many Important Things to WEED OUT the Unbelievers, even as it should be: beCause Jehovah God does not Want any Unbelievers in his Holy Kingdom; but, he Wants Honest MEN, who will Love and OBEY him, who might have to be Born as Women, several Times, just to become Good Men, when they are Born Again in New Bodies: beCause there is such a Thing as Reincarnation, which merely Means "the Re-entering of a Spirit into a Body," and nothing more. Therefore, when Jesus was Resurrected, his Spirit was Reincarnated, which was also True of every Person who was Resurrected: beCause it is Impossible to have a Resurrection without the Act of Reincarnation! †‡

01-06 [_] O Good Pastor of Uncommon Sense, how come those Verses are not Highlighted in RED with Diamond-ratings, like so many of your other Verses in: "Is America a White Nation with a Black Heart?" (How to Separate Truth from Fiction!) **By** The Good Pastor of Uncommon Sense! Book 118, and in: "Which Church is the Right Church?" (Can all Churches be Correct?) **By** The Good Pastor of Uncommon Sense! Book 119?

01-07 [_] Well, my Friend, all of the Verse Numbers and Boxes, which are Highlighted in Red, must be Checked by the Readers who have Intentions of Joining: "The New RIGHTEOUS One-World Government!" (HOW to Establish a Righteous One-World Government without Going to WAR!) By The Worldwide People's

Revolution!® Book 056, who must Check the Boxes with Statements that they Agree with, with DARK GREEN-X Marks, while Checking the Boxes with Statements that they Disagree with, with LARGE RED-X Marks, whereby the Computers can Sort Out the Intelligent People from the Ignorant Fools. For Example, …

A-[_] I Agree that there used to be Giants on the Earth: beCause the *Holy Bible* and other Books say so; but, more than that, there is much Physical Evidence for it — such as the GIANT STONES that are set up all around the World, which one can Discover on the Internet, by Searching in YouTube Videos; or, by Visiting Places — such as Jerusalem, which has Giant Stones in the Foundations, one of which is 11 feet High, 14 feet Wide and 60 feet Long, which Weighs more than 640 Tons, which was Set in Place by the GIANTS, or at least by Heavy CRANES, which Stones were Moved there from a Rock Quarry that is more than 200 Miles away from there! But, you are Welcome to Ignore the Facts: beCause God does not Want any Unbelievers in his Holy Kingdom, which will Exclude U.

B-[_] I do not Believe in Giants. There were NO Giants on the Earth, ever. †§‡

C-[_] I Confess that there might have been Giants during Ancient Times; but, God is NOT a Giant: beCause, Jesus said so! Indeed, he said, *"The Most High God is a Great SPIRIT Being, who Livz everywhere, whom no Man has ever Seen with his Eyeballs; nor can he be Seen: beCause he is the Invisible God; and they who Worship him, must Worship him in Spirit, and According to the Inspired Words of Provable Truths."* — *The New MAGNIFIED Version (NMV) of John 4:24; First Timothy 1:17; Isaiah 57:15; Matthew 15:8—9; and Related Scriptures.*

D-[_] You can Keep your Dumbass False Religion: beCause I Want nothing to Do with it.

E-[_] Educated People keep an Open, Teachable Mind: beCause they Realize just how Ignorant that they are, who always have New and Wonderful Things to Learn.

F-[_] I Fail to Understand what this Survey is all about. Which Boxes should I Check?

G-[_] God Knows that you were not Born to be a Master; but, only a Servant. Nevertheless, it is also Good for the Servants to Learn what the Master Plan of the Master Farmer is all about, whereby they will not be taken by Surprise when he Appears in the Awesome Dark ROLLING CLOUDS of a FEARSOME SKY, along with his Hosts of Flying Saucers, whose Pilots will be Sweeping Up the Innocent Souls, to take them to Mount Zion: beCause the Outside of the Earth must be Cleansed by Devouring FIRE, which will Reach to the Foundations of the Mountains, just to Cleanse the Good Earth from all of the Abominations of Unclean Men, who had their Priorities Totally Out of Order, who did not even Understand WHY that they were Born into this World of Wonders! ‡

H-[_] To be Perfectly Honest with you, this Religious Stuff is far too Sticky for me to Eat.

I-[_] Innocent-minded People will Love it, and Feast on it, Daily, until they Discover **"An Amazing Collection of Wit and Wisdom!" (The Marvelous Tale of the Colorful Peacock from Angel Ridge, and the Strong Rope of Everlasting Hope!) By The Worldwide People's Revolution!®** Book 048.

J-[_] Jesus Warned us to be Aware of False Prophets, who would Come in his Name, saying that he is in Deed the True Christ, or the Anointed One; but, that they would Teach all Kinds of Lies for the Sake of Ungodly Gain: beCause of having their Hearts Set on the Vain Things of this World, on Worldly Riches, which cannot Satisfy the Soul by any Means. Yes, such is the False Prophet from Angel Ridge, at King's Mountain, Kentucky 40442 U.S.A., who Wrote: **"SEVEN TRUMPETS — The Marvelous Tale of the Colorful Peacock, and the Strong Rope of Everlasting Hope!"** which consists of Seven Primary Trumpets, Seven Spiritual Trumpets, Seven Trumpets for Children, Seven Trumpets for Young People, Seven Trumpets for Adults, Seven Trumpets for Old People, and Seven Trumpets to all of the World, which makes 49 Trumpets, which are Crowned with the Trumpet of JUBILEE! Therefore, there are 50 Trumpets, which are Called the Tale Feathers of the Colorful Peacock, who Wrote all 50 Trumpets in just 50 Days, which makes up a Marvelous Book of 1,240 Pages, which was the First Inspired Book that was Written by our Selected

King, which will be the Last of his Books to be Published: beCause, *"The Last shall be First, and the First shall be Last,"* as Jesus stated. †§‡§§

K-[_] King Jesus did not Mention any such Colorful Peacock, nor any such Uninspired Books, which are just Trash Literature, when Compared with *"To Kill a Mockingbird," "The Old Man and the Sea," "The Adventures of Tom Sawyer,"* and *"The Adventures of Huckleberry Finn,"* by Master Mark Twain, who was and still is America's Greatest Author. †§‡

L-[_] Lots of Laughs! Our Selected King is the Reincarnation of Mark Twain and King Solomon, himself! †§‡

M-[_] I would Bet any Amount of Money that you cannot Prove it.

N-[_] Not all Things can be Proven; but, that is Extremely Easy to Prove: beCause it is Proven by the Fact that our Selected King has the Inspired Books to Prove it. For Example, just Read: "Thu Nq MAGNUFIID Verzhun uv Thu PROVERBZ uv KING SOLUMUN in Plaan Ingglish!" (The Understandable Version of the Famous Proverbs of King Solomon in Plain English!) By The Worldwide People's Revolution!® Book 028, which is a Companion Book of: "ECCLESIASTES Uncovered and Recovered!" (The New MAGNIFIED Version of Ecclesiastes and the Song of Solomon in Plain English!) By The Worldwide People's Revolution!® Book 034. Yes, he is the Inspired Author of more than 350 Exceptionally Good Books — all of which are much Better than anything that was ever written by Earnest Hymnalessway, who Failed to Believe in the Gods, and especially in the Most High God, whose Name is Keeoojum, which Means the SUPREME RULER of All Supreme Rulers: beCause, each Galaxy has a Supreme Ruler; and the Supreme Ruler of this Galaxy is Moklom, whose Great Throne is found in the Solar System of Orion. †§‡

O-[_] Are there no Options to Choose from? Must we Check the Boxes with Statements that we Agree with, or Disagree with?

P-[_] Wise People will not Check any Boxes with Permanent Ink, until they have Carefully "Red" all of the Inspired Books of the Colorful Peacock from Angel Ridge, whereby they might Riitlee Juj them; but, they will only Check the Boxes with Led Pencils, whereby they might Erase their Check Marks, later on, if they Change their Minds; and then, they will Use Permanent Ink to Check the Boxes, when they are Ready to become Leaders in: **"The United States of the Whole World!" (A True Global Economy for the Masses of Working People!) By The Worldwide People's Revolution!®** Book 055, which will be Governed by: **"The New RIGHTEOUS One-World Government!" (HOW to Establish a Righteous One-World Government without Going to WAR!) By The Worldwide People's Revolution!®** Book 056, which will Build: **"The Great World TEMPLE of PEACE!" (The Glory of Jerusalem Arises Again in the Great State of Flexible Texas!) By The Worldwide People's Revolution!®** Book 017B, which will be in the Middle of: **"A New Jerusalem in the Great State of Flexible Texas!" (HOW to make Good Use of the Mississippi River!) By The Worldwide People's Revolution!®** Book 090, which will Consist of Believers from all around the World, who will Study: **"HOW to Become a HOLY Man!" (40 Good Reasons WHY People Should FAST and PRAY!) By The Worldwide People's Revolution!®** Book 045, which is a Companion Book of: **"The Proper RULES for FASTING!" (The Complete Instruction Manual for True Repentance!) By The Worldwide People's Revolution!®** Book 046, which is a Companion Book of: **"The Gospel According to our Elected King!" (The Good News from the Most Modern Perspective!) By The Worldwide People's Revolution!®** Book 077, which contains the Famous Sermon that Jonah gave to the People of Nineveh, whereby more than 120,000 People Repented at the same Time, by Fasting and Praying for 40 Consecutive Nights and Days, whereby they were Saved from all of their Dietary Sins and all other Sins, whereby they were Spiritually and Physiologically Born Again! But, you do not have to Believe it to be Saved from all of your Sins: beCause, you only need to Say, "Oh Lordy, Iiz Bleevz in yu," even as Nigger Jim might say to Huck Finn, while Floating Down the Mississippi River on a Raft, during a Full Moonlit Night, in August. Indeed, it is all Fiction, you might say; but, our Selected King makes it come Alive! †§‡§§

Q-[_] The Great Question is this: **"Does Jehovah God Require that every Potential Ruler in the Holy Kingdom of the Great Messiah, must Study all such Inspired Books, just to QUALIFY for Positions within his Great Kingdom?"** And the Answer is: YES!

R-[_] When would we Potential Rulers find TIME to Reed all such Inspired Books? †§‡

S-[_] All of the Saints make Time for Reading those Extremely Good Books, rather than Waste their Precious Time with Television Nonsense, Sports, Eating, and Drinking Booze: beCause they Understand *"HOW to Get our PRIORITIES in ORDER!" (The Glories of Democracy: and, Does DEMON-ocracy have its Priorities in Order?) By The Worldwide People's Revolution!®* Book 060, which is Possible for all True Saints. †§‡

T-[_] I am Most-Interested in that 120-feet-long Circumcised Tally Whacker, and those Chime Bells that are bigger than 55-gallon Oil Barrels! Yes, that has gotten my Attention! Indeed, even Tom Sawyer and Huck Finn would also be Interested; but, not that Nigger Jim: beCause he is already Puffed Up with Great Pride over his own Tally Whacker. †§‡§§

U-[_] I Understand that God does Things in Strange Ways; but, this is just Far too Strange for me to Accept, and Especially the Evil Things that can be found in: **"How GAY is GOD?" (Oh, the Wonders of it all, when it ALL Hangs Out!) By The Worldwide People's Revolution!®** Book 071. Indeed, no one in his nor her Riit Mind could Accept all such Strange Words, unless he is GAY, in which Case he would have to Confess that Jehovah God will get the Last Laugh! But, that is not to say that God is a Sodomite, just beCause he is GAY: beCause, for Example, King David was a Man after God's own Heart, and he Loved Jonathan more than any Womb-man: beCause Jonathan Loved him far more than any Womb-man, according to *Second Samuel 1:26,* which is most likely the Truth of it: beCause, who on this Good Earth was Built Better than King David, who Slew a Lion and a Bear, and Leaped Over a Tall Stone Wall with his Sword in Hand? (See *First Samuel 17.*) Indeed, there are far too many Unsolved Mysteries in that Unholy Mutilated Bible, which Need to be Clarified, at: "The

GREAT Worldwide TELEVISED Court HEARING!" (That Great Meeting of the Most-Intelligent and Well-Educated Minds!) By The Worldwide People's Revolution!® Book 041B, if God does not Object to it; and I cannot Understand WHY he would Object to it, since he Loves TRUTHS! †§‡§§

V-[_] Faith is the VICTORY, my Friend. Therefore, we must have LOTS of Faith in Provable Truths; but, no Faith in Provable Lies — such as People going to Heaven when they Die: beCause, Jesus said, *No Man on this Good Earth has Ascended Up to Heaven, to the Throne of the Most-High God at any Time, except for the Chosen Son of the Most-High God of this Solar System, who Transported him to that Heavenly Place in his Great Spaceship, in a matter of Seconds: beCause the Gods know how to Travel at Lightning Speeds, by Faith! Yes, it is a Mystery to you, even as it should be: beCause, why should People be Traveling all about in the Vast Universe, when they are not Able to Manage their own Lives, right here on the Earth? Would they also take their False Doctrines to other Worlds, and Contaminate them with their Abominations? Therefore, People should Study the Purpose for which they were Born here, to Learn their Spiritual Lessons, whereby they might Qualify for some Positions in the Kingdom of God, if they Pass all of their Tests, and Overcome all of their Sins, and Stop Sinning! After all, the Gods do not Want any Unholy People in their Great Kingdoms, and neither do I Want any such Evil People in my Great Kingdom, which will be Established at the End of the Ages, after all of you have Learned your Lessons, if that is Possible. Most People would say that it is Impossible; but, with God, all Good Things are Possible for those Wise People, who Believe and Obey all of my Commandments, who Think no Evil, who Seek All that is GOOD, and Especially the Goodness of those* "GLORIOUS Swanky Hotels Castles and Fortresses!" (Beautiful Planned City States for WISE Intelligent Well-Educated People with Common Sense and Good Understanding!) By The Worldwide People's Revolution!® Book 019B: beCause, there are more than 5,000 Advantages for Building them and Living within the Borders of them, which is Explained in: "The Right Design for Living!" (A List of Great Advantages for Building Beautiful Planned City States!) By The Worldwide People's Revolution!® Book 012B, which is a Companion Book of: "The Low Court of Supreme Injustices is Brought to Trial!" (Our Selected King Butts Heads with the United States Supreme Court, with or without their Black Robes of Hypocrisies and Lies!) By The Worldwide People's Revolution!® Book 011B, which is a Companion Book of: "**Poverty Hunger Riots Strikes Police Brutalities Election Deceptions and Civil Wars!**" (**The High Price that we Earthlings have Paid for Leaving the Good Land!**) **By The Worldwide People's Revolution!®** Book 014B, which is a Companion Book of: "**Seven Great Armies of Working Soldiers!**" (**HOW to Provide a Way for Everyone to WORK: so as to Eliminate Poverty, Crimes, Drug Abuses, Prisons and Unnecessary Taxes!**) **By The Worldwide People's Revolution!®** Book 015B, which is a Companion Book of: "Does a Good Soldier have to be a MURDERER!" (Seven Great Swanky Armies of Voluntary Working Soldiers!) By The Worldwide People's Revolution!® Book 027B, which is a Companion Book of: "**The Swanky Associations of Working Soldiers!**" (**A Fascinating Collection of Various Kinds of Voluntary Working Soldiers!**) **By The Worldwide People's Revolution!®** Book 018B, which is a Companion Book of: "**101 Good Reasons and Great Advantages for Establishing a Righteous One-World Government!**" (**Government By the People, Of the People, and For the People!**) **By The Worldwide People's Revolution!®** Book 104, which is a Companion Book of: "HOW to Make America (and all other Nations) Really GREAT Without Telling any LIES!" (The Founding Fathers would have Loved it!) By The Worldwide People's Revolution!® Book 092, which is a Companion Book of: "**Provable Truths that True Christians cannot Rightly Deny!**" (A Fair Challenge for all Professing "Christians" to Meditate on with Honest Open Minds!) By The Worldwide People's Revolution!® Book 086, which is a Companion Book of: "All of the Arguments are in Favor of our Selected King, who has Zero Challengers!" (Before you Attend another Election Deception, you should Carefully Study this Inspired Book with an Honest Open Mind!) By The Worldwide People's Revolution!® Book 085.

W-[_] Many People will Prefer to go to WAR, than to Build those "Beautiful Swanky Stone Dome Home COMPLEXES!" (HOW to Build SECURE Tax-proof, Insurance-proof, Self-air-conditioned, Paint-proof, Rot-proof, Termite-proof, Mouse-proof, Fireproof, Tornado-proof, Hurricane-proof, Thief-proof, and BOMB-PROOF Houses!) By The Worldwide People's Revolution!® Book 102, within: "Beautiful Swanky PALACES!" (A New Concept in Living Habits — Swanky Palaces for Poor People!) By The Worldwide People's Revolution!® Book 066: beCause they Suffer with Chronic Constipation of their Minds, whereby they cannot Think Straight. Therefore, they should have to Fill Out and File: "The Complete SURVEYS of our VALUES!" (SURVEYS of Religious Spiritual Political Governmental Sexual Social Moral Economical Business Labor Habitual and Miscellaneous VALUES!) By The Worldwide People's Revolution!® Book 059, just to Discover whether or not they are CRAZY!

X-[_] X-number of People have no Idea what is Good for them: beCause they have not even Studied, "The Simplistic SURVEYS of our VALUES!" Book 059B.

Y-[_] I am Yearning for the Happy Day when we will never have to Reed another Bouk, even if all of the Spelling is Correct: beCause, I am too Lazy to Read Books. †§‡§§

Z-[_] Even the Stubborn Zebras will be Happy to Reed the Inspired Bouks of the Colorful Peacock from Angel Ridge: beCause they are more Interesting than anything in the Unholy Mutilated Bibles, which no Sane Person could Tolerate for very long: beCause of the Multitude of Ridiculous Contradictions. †§‡

01-08 [_] O Good Pastor of Uncommon Sense, I Prefer to Hide myself in this Concrete Jungle. †§

01-09 [_] Well, my Friend, you might Hide yourself for a while; but, you can be Sure that "the Beast" will be Working Hard to get you Branded with the Marks or Numbers of the Beast, who Wants Total Control over everyone, whereby no one is Free: beCause it is an Edomite Slavery System, whereby almost everyone is made into an Education Slave, just to Obtain an Edomite Diploma from "The Public School of IGNERUNT FQLZ!" (HOW we have been GRAATLEE DISEEVD by Capitalism!) By The Worldwide People's Revolution!® Book 024B, whereby a Person might Obtain a so-called "Good Job," whereby a Person might Earn enough Money for making himself into a Work

Slave, Tax Slave, Insurance Slave, Rent Slave, Home-owner Slave, Interest Slave, Credit Card Debt Slave, ElecTrickery Bills Slave, Food Bills Slave, Water Bills Slave, Gas Bills Slave, Transportation Bills Slave, Repair Bills Slave, Entertainment Bills Slave, Drug Bills Slave, Doctor Bills Slave, Hospital Bills Slave, Childcare Bills Slave, Telephone Bills Slave, Internet Bills Slave, Mortgage Bills Slave, Nursing Home Bills Slave, Funeral Home Bills Slave, and Endless Bills SLAVE: beCause that is the Objective of those Lying Conniving Edomites, who never tell their Slaves that it is Possible and most Practical to have NO SLAVERY AT ALL! Moreover, this Inspired Book Reveals HOW to Manage that, which is WHY this Book is so Hated by those Edomite Bank Robbers, who have Gained TRILLIONS of Dollars by Means of their Slavery Systems, and especially by Means of those Hateful WARS: beCause they Cheerfully Loan Money to both Sides of the War Games, and Collect Interest or Usury on their Loans. Yes, it Reminds me of a Sign over the Doorway of a certain Office in Danville, Kentucky, which red: FOX and CROW — Money to Loan; and, by Working Together, they "Fleeced" X-number of Ignorant Sheeps and Goats, who Lost their Houses, their Farms, their Vehicles, their Furniture, and whatever they Borrowed Money for, to Buy, according to the Fox and Crow Plan, which was nothing but an Edomite Scam, which could not Function without the FALSE OWNERSHIP DOCTRINE of Satan, the Devil, who Uses that Doctrine to make X-number of SLAVES: beCause, if all People just put that False Doctrine into the Trash Can, like the First Christians did, those Lying Conniving Edomites would go Out of Business! Yes, it is all Explained in: "The New MAGNIFIED Version of the Book of ACTS!" (The Understandable Version of the Acts of the Apostles in Plain English!) By The Worldwide People's Revolution!® Book 063, which Unravels the Mystery as to WHY the Jews Hated Christ and his Disciples so much that they Sought to Destroy them! Yes, Paul used to be Saul, who went about Persecuting the Christians at the Command of those Jews in Jerusalem, who saw the Christians as a Great Threat to their Evil Empire: beCause they Trashed the Ownership Doctrine, and went about Selling everything that they Possessed: so that they might Pool their Resources, and Build a Beautiful Planned City State, without any Loans, without any Interest / Usury, without any Taxes, and without any Bankers, which really Disturbed those Edomites: beCause they were the Chief Bankers, who made their Living by LOANING MONEY to Ignorant People, who did not Understand the Edomite Scam! ‡

01-10 [_] O Good Pastor of Uncommon Sense, are you saying that it might be Possible to Liv a Healthy Happy Life without any Hateful

Bankers, just by Trashing the False Ownership Doctrine? For Example, HOW would I Build or Buy a House, if I could not Use the Services of a Bank? †§‡

— Chapter 02 —

Will there be any Banks and Bankers in Heaven?

02-01 [_] "The New RIGHTEOUS One-World Government!" (HOW to Establish a Righteous One-World Government without Going to WAR!) By The Worldwide People's Revolution!® Book 056, will simply Obey: "The CONSTITUTION for the New RIGHTEOUS One-World Government!" (HOW all Peoples can get True Justice, and Celebrate the Great Year of JUBILEE!) By The Worldwide People's Revolution!® Book 016B, which Reveals that a Righteous Government has the Power to Mint and Print the Necessary New Money — NOT to Give it away to Ignorant Fools, nor to Waste it on Needless Bankers; but, to Use that New Money WISELY, in Order to HIRE: "Seven Great Armies of Working Soldiers!" (HOW to Provide a Way for Everyone to WORK: so as to Eliminate Poverty, Crimes, Drug Abuses, Prisons and Unnecessary Taxes!) By The Worldwide People's Revolution!® Book 015B, in Order to Build those "GLORIOUS Swanky Hotels Castles and Fortresses!" (Beautiful Planned City States for WISE Intelligent Well-Educated People with Common Sense and Good Understanding!) By The Worldwide People's Revolution!® Book 019B, which will Represent that New Money, which must be EARNED by Honest Labor, without any Loans, without any Interest, and without any Taxes, according to: "A List of FAIR Swanky Wages!" (The Equitable Wage System!) By The Worldwide People's Revolution!® Book 065: beCause, everyone who Joins "The Swanky Associations of Working Soldiers!" (A Fascinating Collection of Various Kinds of Voluntary Working Soldiers!) By The Worldwide People's Revolution!® Book 018B, has Agreed to Learn, Believe, Love and OBEY: "The New MAGNIFIED Version of the 20 Commandments," which anyone can Discover in: "LIGHTNING STRIKES Versus Lightning Bugs!" (HOW you can Become Moderately RICH, without Telling any Lies nor Selling any Trash!) By The Worldwide People's Revolution!® Book 074, whereby there will be no Need for Police DEPARTments: beCause each

Person will Police himself, or else be BANISHED from those Swanky Fortresses, whereby they will no longer be a Problem for anyone to Solve, who can Liv in the Wilderness with the Snakes, Wolves, Lions, Bears, Scorpions, Chiggers, Ticks, Bedbugs, Fleas, Mosquitoes, and whatever Evil Creatures Liv in the Wilderness, who might Torment them. For Example, a Person could Plant an Acre of Sweet Corn, and not get so much as one Cob of Corn to Eat: beCause of being Raided by a Herd of Raccoons, of a hundred or more, who would Plan on their Attack. For Example, I had a Naaber on Angel Ridge, who Planted his Sweet Corn, which certain Raccoons were keeping an Eye on, as well as the entire Family. Therefore, when they all got up and went to Church, one Sunday Morning, a certain Raccoon Called for the other Raccoons, and more than 100 of them Suddenly Appeared from the Woods, and Raided that Corn Patch, and never left even one Cob for that Family to EAT! I Mean that they Wiped it OUT! Yes, they were Extremely Well-Organized Raccoons, who had Learned HOW to Do it, who also knew how to Communicate with one another, whose Elders were Leading and Teaching the Younger ones HOW to Do it, and not get Caught; but, I was Watching them at a Distance, and got to Witness the Thievery, first-hand; but, I did not have a Camera, much less, an iPhone with a Movie Camera: beCause, in 1973, they did not have any such Telephones. Nevertheless, I Thot to myself, "How could a Gardener Prevent any such Things as that, while Living so Close to the Forest?" And the Holy Spirit said to me, "There is only one Rational Solution, called Beautiful Swanky Fortresses, which will not only Solve that Problem; but, will also Solve thousands of other Problems." †§‡§§

02-02 |_| And, being very Ignorant, I Asked: "Pray tell, what would that Solution be?" And the Holy Spirit Answered, "The People would have to Act Wisely, and Pool their Resources to Build Beautiful Planned City States, in Great Stone Terraces, which Cities are Protected by Deep Moats that Surround them, and Tall Stone Walls that no Raccoons can Climb Over: beCause of being Designed to Keep them Out." And I said, "But, how could they ever Afford to Build any such Beautiful Planned City States, which would Cost Trillions of Dollars?" And she said, "That is the Reason for Establishing a Righteous One-World Government, which has an Unlimited Supply of Good Money, which must be Earned by Honest Labor, without any Loans, without any Usury, and without any Taxes." And I said, "Are you saying that such a Good Government would simply Hire Young Men to Build such Cities, and the Stonework would Represent that New Money?" And she said, "Yes, that is Exactly what I am saying. Moreover, there is no Need for anyone making a Slave of himself, just to Liv in a Beautiful Stone Dome Home: beCause, all such Stone Dome Homes can Belong to the Eternal Righteous Government, which cannot Die, if it is Maintained according to a Good Constitution. Therefore, I Want you to Write that Good Constitution for these Ignorant People, who might Happen to Reed it, once that they have Suffered Long Enough as SLAVES, whereby they might Sacrifice the Ownership Doctrine of the Devil on the Altar of True Love, whereby they might Help one another to Build those Beautiful Planned City States for their Righteous One-World Government, which must also Love them, and do its Best to Help them to Prosper, by making Mechanical Slaves to Assist them: beCause they will Need Mountains of Cut and Polished Stones to Work with, as well as Sand and Gravel for making Concrete with Cement and Water. Therefore, it is your Duty to Persuade these Ignorant People to Believe and Obey your Constitution and the Commandments of God, who now Commands them to Build those Beautiful Planned City States, whereby they can Solve thousands of Problems!" And I said, "But, those Boneheads will not Listen to me: beCause I do not have any Diplomas, to Prove that I am Educated." And she said, "Do not Fret yourself over it: beCause, it is not by Might, nor by Power; but, it is According to my Holy Spirit, says the Supreme Ruler and Divine Lawmaker. Therefore, have Faith in All that is Good, and Write the Books that I will Inspire you with: beCause, you will not Finish Writing all of those Exceptionally Good Books, before the End of Confusion will Come, and Babylon will Fall." Therefore, there will be no Banks nor Bankers in Heaven: beCause, the Earth will be made into a Heavenly Place for everyone to Liv, just by Establishing **"The New RIGHTEOUS One-World Government!" (HOW to Establish a Righteous One-World Government without Going to WAR!) By The Worldwide People's Revolution!®** Book 056.‡

02-03 [_] O Good Pastor of Uncommon Sense, I can Hear what you are Saying, and it Sounds very Good to me; but, I Seriously Doubt that the Masses of People will Give Up their False Ownership Doctrine, and put their Trust in a Righteous One-World Government, which will have Total Control over them, whereby they will Lose all of their Freedoms, just as soon as your Selected King DIES and goes to Heaven, or perhaps to Hell, just for telling so many Outlandish Lies — such as Jehovah God Living Inside of Jupiter! Therefore, how can we Solve that Problem? †§‡§§

02-04 [_] Well, my Friend, you are Inventing a Problem that does not even Exist, and will never Exist, if our Selected King is ever Elected: beCause, once those **"GLORIOUS Swanky Hotels Castles and Fortresses!" (Beautiful Planned City States for WISE Intelligent**

Well-Educated People with Common Sense and Good Understanding!) By The Worldwide People's Revolution!® Book 019B, are Constructed, they will Govern themselves: beCause they will have no Need for any Monster Federal Government: beCause, everyone will be Set Up Properly for LIVING, at Home, with large All-Mineral Organic Gardens, which are Attended to by **"The Swanky Association of Professional Organic Gardeners,"** who will have Rich, 3-feet-deep Topsoil to Work in, with "Profitable Swanky MULCHING ROCKS!" (30 Advantages for Using Swanky Mulching Rocks in an All-Mineral Organic Garden!) By The Worldwide People's Revolution!® Book 098. Nevertheless, just to make Sure that no Tyrants Arise among those Swanky Fortresses, they must be Watched by Voluntary Newsmen, who can Liv and Work within each Planned City State, and Report whatever is going on, in:

Book 030-0002, which everyone will be Welcome to Contribute to: beCause the Primary Branch of "The New RIGHTEOUS One-World Government!" (HOW to Establish a Righteous One-World Government without Going to WAR!) By The Worldwide People's Revolution!® Book 056, is the NEWS MEDIA, which must be made up of RIGHTEOUS People, who are Working for the Masses of People, and not for the Government, which will have its own Good News Reporters, who will be telling about all of the Good Things that are going on at Swanky Fortresses; but, not Outside of them: beCause that will be the Duty of Independent News Reporters and Whistleblowers, who will be Reporting their Bad News to the People who Liv Outside of Swanky Fortresses, who may also Listen to the News that is Reported to the People who Liv within those Swanky Fortresses, which will be very GOOD News, which will Encourage those Outsiders to Move into Swanky Fortresses, just to Solve their Problems. For Example, if People are Worried about Dying from some Bug or Germ, they only have to Visit one of those "Beautiful Swanky FASTING SANITARIUMS!" (HOW to Learn Good Self-Discipline!) **By** The Worldwide People's Revolution!® Book 115, whereby they can get Rid of the Morbid Stuff that Viirusez and Germs of all Kinds Grow in, which they will easily Understand when they Study: "The Proper RULES for FASTING!" (The Complete Instruction Manual for True Repentance!) By The Worldwide People's Revolution!® Book 046. Therefore, you can get the Head-start on them. †‡

02-05 |_| O Good Pastor of Uncommon Sense, are you Sure that Swanky Fortresses will not get Corrupted by Wicked People, who are Attending to their All-Mineral Organic Gardens? For Example, while their Elected

Kings and Queens are Working in their Vineyards, Vegetable Gardens, Orchards, and Home-craft Workshops, those Niggers will be figuring out how to Sell Drugs, to get more Money: so that they can Buy Limousines to go Shopping for Bananas, or something that is Sold at the General Stores, which cannot be Found in their Gardens, even though it will be Possible and far more Practical for them to Telephone a Delivery Boy, who can bring the Bananas to them in a Quadracycle, along with whatever their Naaberz Order, at the same Time: beCause that Service will be somewhat like Amazon, which will Deliver whatever you Want; but, for Free: beCause all of the Members of "The Swanky Associations of Working Soldiers!" (A Fascinating Collection of Various Kinds of Voluntary Working Soldiers!) By The Worldwide People's Revolution!® Book 018B, put in their 3 to 4 Hours of Common Skilled Labor, and then have the Remainder of the Day Off: so that they can Eat at one of those "Royal Swanky Buffets!" (The Best Feasts in the Whole World!) By The Worldwide People's Revolution!® Book 103, and then go to a Theater to Watch a Good Educational Movie; or else go to Church Services, or do whatever they Like: beCause they will all have 20 Hours of the Day to Do whatever they Want to: beCause they Sacrifice 4 Hours in Exchange for Living like Rich People, within those "Beautiful Swanky PALACES!" (A New Concept in Living Habits — Swanky Palaces for Poor People!) By The Worldwide People's Revolution!® Book 066, which none of them could Afford to Buy; but, there is no Need for Buying them, and making Slaves of themselves, just to Eat and Drink and Wear some Rags, and "VOTE for The GOAT!" (The New Political Party that has Guaranteed Solutions for our Massive Problems!) By The Worldwide People's Revolution!® Book 109: beCause, there will be no Need for any more Election Deceptions, once everyone is Set Up Properly for LIVING, at Home! Indeed, if you Need some Special Tool to Work with, just go to the Swanky Tool House, and Borrow it, Free of all Charges: beCause that is the Reason for having a GOOD Tool House, which has every Useful Tool that one can Think of, which also has a Machine Shop for Making Special Tools, if they are Needed. Likewise, if you Want a Musical Instrument to Play, you only need to Visit the Music Shop, which will have Music Teachers: beCause they put in their 4 Hours as Music Teachers, whereby they Contribute to the Swanky Fortress System. Otherwise, if they have no Students, they can Attend to their Gardens, and Liv in their "Beautiful Swanky Stone Dome Home COMPLEXES!" (HOW to Build SECURE Tax-proof, Insurance-proof, Self-air-conditioned, Paint-proof, Rot-proof, Termite-proof, Mouse-proof, Fireproof, Tornado-proof, Hurricane-proof, Thief-proof, and BOMB-PROOF Houses!) By The Worldwide People's Revolution!® Book 102: beCause no one is under any Capitalist Pressure to get anything Done; but, they all *"Do with all of their Might, whatsoever their Hands Discover to Do, as if Doing it for God, and not for People: beCause they all Love their Naaberz just as much as they Love themselves,"* which is the Christian Way of Doing it. But, if someone does not Like the Christian Way of Doing it, they are Welcome to Invent their own Ways of Doing whatever they Do; but, only with other People of Like-mindedness: beCause, Good Honest Hardworking People are not going to be Taxed to Support Lazy Sloths, nor Crazy Selfish Hogs, who are Welcome to Liv with other Crazy Selfish Hogs, until they become Sick of themselves, and Decide to Change their Minds, and Adopt the Christian Ways of Doing Things. ‡

02-06 |_| Well, my Friend, that Sounds Good Enough for me: beCause everyone will be Free, with no more Hateful Bills to Pay, and hardly any Trash in the Trash Dump: beCause everyone will have a Silver Spoon to Eat their Cantaloupes and Watermelons; and they will Keep their Spoons in their own Pockets, and Wash them after Eating. Therefore, no one will be Tempted to Steal a Silver Spoon, nor Mistreat it: beCause it will be their Responsibility to take Good Care of their own Spoons, Combs, Swiss Army Knives, Tooth Brushes, Ink Pens, and whatever they have in their own Private Pockets, including their iPhones, which will be the Best in the World; and everyone can have one, for Free: beCause X-number of People will Volunteer to Make them, for Free, for the Love of their Naaberz, who will also Volunteer 4 Hours per Workday to Do whatever they are Asked to Do, even if only to Clean Toilets, Mop Floors, Wash Windows, Hoe Weeds, Pick Fruits, Cook Meals, Sew Clothes, Make Furniture, Assemble Tools, or Do whatever they Volunteer to Do, who will also be Free to Choose their own Masters, and everyone will have a Master, including the Elected King and Queen: beCause, there is "A Sound Argument for Good Masters and Obedient Servants!" (WHY Everyone Needs a Good Master, and every Master Needs Good Obedient Servants!) By The Worldwide People's Revolution!® Book 008B. Yes, it is called Cooperation for the Benefit of Everyone. Therefore, there will be no Poor People among us, unless they Willingly Choose to be Poor, which is a little Stupid: beCause nothing is Gained by it, when it is Possible for everyone to become Moderately Rich in all Ways, being Healthy, Wealthy and WISE. Nevertheless, you must Check the Boxes with Statements that you Agree with, in: "The Complete SURVEYS of our VALUES!" (SURVEYS of Religious Spiritual Political Governmental Sexual Social Moral Economical Business Labor Habitual and Miscellaneous VALUES!) By The Worldwide People's Revolution!®

Book 059, whereby the Computers can Assist you to Discover other People of Like-mindedness, whom you can Love and Respect. †§‡§§

02-07 [_] O Good Pastor of Uncommon Sense, if the Masses of People Learn the Whole Truth about each Important Subject, there is a Good Chance that everyone will come up with the same Happy Conclusion, which is to make a Paradise on the Earth for everyone who is Willing to Cooperate with: "The New RIGHTEOUS One-World Government!" (HOW to Establish a Righteous One-World Government without Going to WAR!) By The Worldwide People's Revolution!® Book 056, which will not even Construct its own Constitution, until after we have Conducted: "The GREAT Worldwide TELEVISED Court HEARING!" (That Great Meeting of the Most-Intelligent and Well-Educated Minds!) By The Worldwide People's Revolution!® Book 041B, whereby we might all Learn what is Good for us, and then Decide to "VOTE for The GOAT!" (The New Political Party that has Guaranteed Solutions for our Massive Problems!) By The Worldwide People's Revolution!® Book 109, who will Accept all of the Blame for whatever goes WRong, after we put him in Charge of that Good Government, who will be Wise, and Cause each Group of Wise People to Elect their own Leaders, whereby they can only Blame themselves for whatever goes WRong. However, if they get into Trouble, they can always Call on "The New RIGHTEOUS One-World Government!" (HOW to Establish a Righteous One-World Government without Going to WAR!) By The Worldwide People's Revolution!® Book 056, whose Headquarters will be in: "The Great World TEMPLE of PEACE!" (The Glory of Jerusalem Arises Again in the Great State of Flexible Texas!) By The Worldwide People's Revolution!® Book 017B, whose Elected Officials will also be taking Care of their own Gardens and Home-craft Workshops, if there is nothing for them to Do, which will eventually be the Case, if Things are Managed Correctly: beCause all of the Wicked People will be Discovered and Eliminated by themselves, who will not Choose to Liv within any of those "GLORIOUS Swanky Hotels Castles nor Fortresses!" (Beautiful Planned City States for WISE Intelligent Well-Educated People with Common Sense and Good Understanding!) By The Worldwide People's Revolution!® Book 019B: beCause they are nothing but Ignorant FOOLS, who will get just Exactly what they Deserve, while the Righteous People will be getting just Exactly what they Deserve, which will be those "Royal Swanky Buffets!" (The Best Feasts in the Whole World!) By The Worldwide People's Revolution!® Book 103, within: "Beautiful Swanky PALACES!" (A New Concept in Living Habits — Swanky Palaces for Poor People!) By The Worldwide People's Revolution!® Book 066, which will Inspire many Outsiders to Move themselves into Swanky Fortresses, until at last, Righteousness will Overcome Wickedness.

02-08 [_] Well, my Friend, it will Prove to be Interesting to See just how it all Turns Out; but, I venture to say that Most People will Agree with you, and Check that Box with a Large Green-X Mark. However, if not, I would say that they are Mentally Ill, being a Trumpite or Edomite, and should Visit one of those: "Swanky Institutions for Compassionate Corrections!" (How to Correct even the Most-Stubborn Bullies!) **By The Biggest Bully of All Bullies! Book 116.** †§‡

02-09 |_| O Good Pastor of Uncommon Sense, if there is anyone who Objects to Conducting: "The GREAT Worldwide TELEVISED Court HEARING!" (That Great Meeting of the Most-Intelligent and Well-Educated Minds!) By The Worldwide People's Revolution!® Book 041B, that Person is Suspect of being an Enemy of Mankind, who should be brought to Court for Questioning: beCause of being a Near Relative of some Hateful Murderous TERRORIST! After all, what is WRong or Bad with Learning the Whole Truth about each Important Subject? ‡

02-10 |_| Well, my Friend, it is Possible that some Simple-minded People do not Understand what such a Meeting of the Minds is all about: beCause of not taking the Time to Study that Inspired Book. Therefore, there is no Need for Wasting anyone's Precious Time, nor Government Money, by bringing them to Court: beCause, they will Eventually Conform to Righteousness, if they are just left alone, whereby they will Meet with their own Fates. After all, God knows how to Humble them in the Right Way to be Corrected. Therefore, just Pray for them, that God will Humble them.‡

— Chapter 03 —

Will Holy Angels be Serving us with Great Banquets?

03-01 [_] I Remember when I was just a little Boy, maybe 8 or 9 Years Old, when I Asked our Mother what we would be Eating when we got to Heaven? And she said something like this: "We will be Eating whatever the Angels Serve to us, and they will also be Washing the Dishes for us." And I said, "Why would they be Doing all of that for us, when we could do it for ourselves?" And she said, "Well, my Son, you will Understand why after 40 Years of Slave Labor." And our Daddy said, "That is Right, my Son, you just have to be Patient, and you will Learn why." So, that Ended that Conversation. However, 60-plus Years Later, I have to Disagree with them: beCause, I am still Able and Willing to Feed myself, and Wash my own Dishes. Nevertheless, I do not Object to Young Voluntary Working Soldiers doing it for themselves and for all of the Old People: beCause, what else would they be Doing, after everyone is Set Up Properly for Living? For Example, the Ceramic Floors might Need some Mopping, once per Month, just to keep them Clean: beCause of Dust Creeping in, somehow; but, that would only Require a couple Hours of Work for some Young Person, who might only have to Mop Floors once per Month, for only 4 Hours: beCause there would be lots of Young People to Do it, if Babies were being Born; and, Ideally, each Family would have 2 Babies, or 3 at the most, unless they were Exceptionally Beautiful People, who would be Encouraged to have more Babies: beCause no one has ever gotten Tired of Looking at Beautiful People, as far as I know. At least I have not. However, if you Want some Really UGLY Children, just Eat all that you might Lust after, at some "Royal Swanky Buffets!" (The Best Feasts in the Whole World!) By The Worldwide People's Revolution!® Book 103. †§‡§§

03-02 [_] O Good Pastor of Uncommon Sense, if Eating too much at a Royal Swanky Buffet could make your Children Ugly, should the Government Set Limits and Regulations on what People Eat? Would that be Freedom, Liberty, and Justice for ALL?

03-03 [_] Well, my Friend, each Person should Regulate himself, once he has become an Adult; but, I would say that it would be a Good Thing to Regulate the Children, at least when they go to School, where they can be Tawt what is Best for them. Nevertheless, it is up to each Swanky

Fortress to Figure it all out: beCause no one Wants nor Needs a Monster Federal Government Managing their Lives, unless they Ask for it; and, even then, it should be Limited. ‡

A-[_] I Agree, the Righteous One-World Government should not be Managing anyone's Life for them, nor Supporting them when they get Sick nor Diseased: beCause it is their Problem — not their Naaber'z Problem. †§‡

B-[_] I Believe that it is the Duty of the Government to Manage our Lives, and take Full Responsibility for us, even if they have to Collect Tax Money to do that. †§‡

C-[_] I Confess that it is a very Complicated Subject, for which there are no Quick, Ready-made Solutions, except to Explain to all of the People that it is their Responsibility to take Good Care of their own Health, and to Eat with Moderation: beCause no one Wants to be Taxed for Medicare, Medicaid, nor any other Kind of Healthcare: beCause Civilized People do not make themselves into Drunkards, Gluttons, Fat Hogs, nor Sodomites, whereby they might Contract Sexual Diseases, which can be Avoided by having Clean Frot Sex, like the Ancient Greeks Practiced, who Avoided Rapes, Murders, Prostitution, Sodomy, and all such Evils, which were Jewish Problems: beCause they did not Teach Men to have Clean Frot Sex, whereby they might be Relieved of their Natural Craving for Sex when they were Teenagers, without making Fools of themselves by Sinning. †§‡

D-[_] Why not use DUMBmocracy to Decide what Regulations should be Imposed on People? After all, if the Majority of the People Vote for Taxing themselves to Support Medical Care, that should be their Decision, as a MOB: beCause Democracy is Mob Rulership, which is a Good Thing, and Especially if you take Good Care of your own Health, whereby you are Able to Work Hard and Save your Money, only to have some Robbing Government take it away from you by FORCE, with a Threat of Time in Prison, if you Fail to Pay your Taxes to People who cannot Manage themselves Properly. †§‡§§

E-[_] Educated People Understand that there are Accidents in this World of Woes, whereby People get Hurt, and maybe Injure their Backs, whereby they Need some Medical Care.

Therefore, there are no other Options, than to Tax the entire Community to Support the Person who Failed to be Careful, and got himself Injured when the Drunk Driver of another Vehicle ran into the Rear End of his Car, and Injured his Back, for Example. †§†§§

F-[_] Swanky Fortresses have no such Vehicles, whereby someone might be Injured by them. Therefore, that Knocks Out that Problem. Nevertheless, that is not to say that some Ignorant Person could not Injure his Back, just by Lifting on something Heavy, when he is not Used to Doing that Lifting. Otherwise, he might just Load a Heavy Rock into a Wheelbarrow, and get it Off Balance, and thus, Injure his Back: beCause a Wheelbarrow must be Balanced, while a 2-Wheeled Cart Balances itself, and is much Safer to Use. †§‡

G-[_] God knows that there are a Million or more Ways to get Hurt while Working. Therefore, everyone Needs to be Covered by Insurance, no matter what: beCause, Chance and Circumstance has Happened to everyone, as King Solomon said. Therefore, we can Try to Do our Best to Work Slowly and Accurately; but, in spite of Doing our Best, someone is Bound to get Injured, and especially if that someone is an Inexperienced Teenager, who is overly Anxious to get something Finished in a Hurry. Therefore, all such Teenagers should have Guardians to take Care of them, and Teach to them HOW to Work Properly, and what Tools to Use for the Jobs that they are Doing. For Example, a Pruning Hook is much Better for Cutting Off little Limbs on a Tree, than a Machete, or Axe, which could easily Chop into someone's Foot or Leg, while the Pruning Hook is Harmless. †§‡

H-[_] To be Perfectly Honest with you, it might be Better to Allow the Fool to Chop into his Leg, whereby he might Learn to be more Careful, the next Time that he Does something with a Tool, and Especially if it is a SHARP Tool, like an Axe, Saw, Scythe, or Machete.‡

I-[_] Innocent People should not Use Dangerous Tools, and Especially if they are Children, who cannot be Expected to Realize the Dangers: beCause they could get Badly Wounded, or even Killed by Powered Tools — such as Meat Grinders, Saw Mills, Chainsaws, and even Lawnmowers. Therefore, if a

Swanky Fortress Decides to Use any such Powered Tools, they should Expect Injuries, and be Set Up for Treating them; but, I would Choose to Liv within a Swanky Fortress that used Human-powered Tools, only — such as a Digging Fork in the Garden, as Opposed to a Powerful and Dangerous Roto-Tiller, which might Chop Off a Foot or Hand. Nevertheless, if someone is Well-Trained to Use a Powered Tool, it can Save a Person from a LOT of Difficult Work. In Fact, while the Poor Gardener is Digging Up his Garden with a Digging Fork, the Man with a Roto-Tiller can Till under Thick Tough Grasses and Weeds on an entire Acre of Land, while the Poor Man is doing only a little Patch that is 10 or so feet square. Therefore, it is Impractical for using a Digging Fork, when you can Use a Remote-controlled Electric Roto-Tiller, which Tills 2 feet Deep and 4 feet Wide, and Kills every Innocent Earthworm in the Garden. †§‡§§

J-[_] Jesus would Plant a Fig Tree, and forget about Eating Onions and Carrots: beCause that would Eliminate the Need for doing any Digging and Tilling, except to Plant the Tree, which would be Good for 100 or more Years to come. Yes, it is called Vertical Farming: beCause the Tree Reaches Up, and can have more than 10,000 Figs on it, in a Space that is only 20 feet square, which would do well to Grow even 2 Bushels of Okra, which can be Grown around the Fig Tree, until it has Grown Up, which can have Figs as Big as a Child's Fist, and not need Cooking, which can be Dried and Vacuum-packed in a Canning Jar. †§‡

K-[_] King Jesus would likely have us Planting Walnut Trees, which might Produce 10 to 40 Bushels of Walnuts to Feast on; but, I Prefer the Sweet Corn, Kale, Pickled Cucumbers, Tomatoes, Onions, and Lettuce, which makes a Fine Fresh Salad with Mashed Avocados.

L-[_] One Large Mango Tree can have as many as 10,000 Mangoes on it, and it only needs to be Planted one Time with a Digging Fork and Shovel, in the Right Climate, which also Needs the Loving Care of Cows, Chickens, and Peacocks, who all seem to get along quite well Together. However, those Cows also Need some Corn to Munch on, if they are going to be Strong enough to Run an Electric Generator for Producing Light at Night, who can be Worked Inside of a Stone Dome, where the Temperature is Regulated by some Wise Master, who takes Good Care of his Livestock, and does not Overwork them, nor Underfeed them. Just one Cow can keep the Lights Running in a House; but, 2 of them will keep the Family Fed with Milk, Cheese and Meat, while Fertilizing the Fruit and Nut Trees.

M-[_] A Good Milk Cow is Better than Money in the Bank, if you also get to Work her Muscles; and a Big Strong Bull can do twice or 3 Times as much Work as the Cow, whereby he can Earn his Keep, who can be Fed under the Apple and Pear Trees; but, the Swanky Fortress would Require some Open Fields for Growing Grasses and Grains to Feed the Bulls; and one Bull can Service 20 Cows with no Problem, and the other Bulls can be Eaten when they are Young, if anyone can Tolerate the Smell of Butchering them. †§‡§§

N-[_] I Prefer to Eat a Moderate Number of RAW NUTS for my Proteins, and also put my own Dung and Piss under the Trees, at the Driplines; but, not anywhere near to the Trunks of the Trees: beCause that might Cause them to get Diseased. Therefore, with just a few Fruit and Nut Trees, I can be Perfectly Healthy and Satisfied with just a Small Vegetable Garden for some Green Leaves. Otherwise, I can Trade a few Nuts with my Naaberz, for some of their Fresh Vegetables, whereby I can Skip the "Royal Swanky Buffets!" (The Best Feasts in the Whole World!) By The Worldwide People's Revolution!® Book 103

O-[_] Are there no Options to Choose from? Suppose we get Tired of Eating Good Wholesome Natural Foods, and want to Indulge in the Flesh Pots of Egypt, just for the Great Pleasure of it — will God not Permit us to Do that? Surely, he is a God of Mercies.‡

P-[_] People are Free to Choose whatever they Like; but, they should have to Liv with other People who Like the same Things, if it is Possible, whereby they are not Picking and Pecking on each other. Therefore, if some Person Changes his Diet, he should also Change his Fortress, and Move in with other People of Like-mindedness, whereby they can get along better, and perhaps Discover Perfect Companions to Liv with. †§‡

Q-[_] The Great Question is this: **"Should People with very Bad Habits be Allowed into any Swanky Fortresses,"** which might give to those Fortresses BAD Names? [_] Yeah or [_] Nay?

R-[_] I say that all Bad People should be Screened OUT of all Swanky Fortresses: beCause the whole Idea is to Provide Ideal Places for People to Liv and Work. Therefore, Reprobates and Rebels are not Welcome at Swanky Fortresses; but, they are Welcome to Liv in any Cities of Confusion that they Like Best. †§‡

S-[_] Saint Peter would call them Wolves in Sheep's Clothing, and have them Cast OUT! After all, it only Requires one Bad Apple to Spoil the entire Box of Apples. Therefore, whatever Beliefs that a Swanky Fortress has, they should Try to Maintain those Beliefs, just to Prove their Goodness or Evilness, which will Eventually be Manifested to Saints. ‡

T-[_] True Christians do not Use Words like "Manifested": beCause that is a Word that only Lawyers would Use, whereby little Children might not Understand it, which is EVIL: beCause all 12-year-old Children should be Able to Understand everything that is Spoken.

U-[_] I Understand the Principle behind the Idea of Establishing Holy Cities; but, in this Day and Age, no such a Thing is Possible: beCause there is far too much Traffic, and Communication is far too Easy, to Maintain any Control over the People, who will be Smuggling Drugs into Swanky Fortresses, which will get all of them Corrupted, and especially if they are Permitted to Grow Marijuana. Therefore, in Order to Reduce Crimes, it is Best to just give everyone Freedom to Sin as much as they Like, until they have had Enough of it to make them Sick of it; and then they can Move into Swanky Forts. †§‡§§

V-[_] Wise People will be Vigilant, and make Sure that their Children are not Consuming any Drugs, even if they must Strap their Buttockses with a Bull Whip: beCause anyone can Liv a Good Long Healthy Happy Life without any Drugs, at all. For Example, our Selected King has never had a Puff on a Cigarette, nor Used any Drugs of any Kinds; and he has no Pains in his entire Body. Therefore, that is the Right Way to Liv, which Saves a LOT of Money, Suffering, Regrets, Treatments, and whatever comes with all such Foolishness. †‡

W-[ ] I would rather Liv in the Wilderness with the Snakes and Skunks, than to Liv in a Swanky Fortress, where I have Endless Bills to Pay, and Work for 16 Hours per Day, 8 Days per Week, and still cannot get Ahead of the Capitalist Game. Besides that, there would be some Tyrant King telling me every Move to make, whereby I would Want to KILL the Son of Satan with **"The Swanky Sword of Divine Truths!"** Book 067. †§‡§§

X-[ ] X-number of Fools will Presume all such Nonsense about Swanky Fortresses, without ever Studying our Selected King's Master Plan, which Calls for Freedom, Liberty and Justice for ALL Peoples, Worldwide, without Exploiting anyone. Therefore, before you Speak Evil of Swanky Fortresses, you should Study the Plan: beCause you might Like it. After all, no less than 6 Billion People Like it; but, they Feel Powerless to Do anything about it: beCause of being so Far into DEBTS. However, all of those Debts can be Forgiven, even as Moses Explained in *Leviticus 25*. Therefore, that is the Right Way to get Rid of those Needless Debts. †§‡

Y-[ ] I would have Believed it, just Yesterday; but, after Learning what the Federal Government has Planned for us, I just Want to Die and go to Heaven!

Z-[ ] The Zeal of "The Worldwide People's Revolution!" (A Comprehensive Plan for Obtaining Worldwide Law, Order, Obedience, Peace and True Prosperity!) By The Worldwide People's Revolution!® Book 108, will Change all of that, and give to you an entire List of Good Reasons to Want to Stick around here: beCause Exciting Times are Coming, when the Earth will be Transformed into: "The Environmentalists' Perfect Paradise!" (HOW almost Everyone can be Living in a Beautiful Manmade Paradise!) By The Worldwide People's Revolution!® Book 035C.

03-04 [ ] O Good Pastor of Uncommon Sense, I Visualize a Heaven with Long Banquet Tables made of Pure Gold, and Covered with Silver Dishes and Large Silver Bowls full of Delicious Foods, which are Grown in Weedless Gardens by Holy Angels, who use "Profitable Swanky

MULCHING ROCKS!" (30 Advantages for Using Swanky Mulching Rocks in an All-Mineral Organic Garden!) By The Worldwide People's Revolution!® Book 098, of Various Colors and Kinds, with Water Fountains and Waterfalls, which run into little Creeks with Colorful Polished Granite Boulders, which are used to Irrigate those Gardens in Underground Ceramic Pipes, which have Leaking Joints every foot, when the Water is Flooded into the Pipes, whereby it Seeps Out through the Joints, and Soaks Up the Topsoil: beCause that will Conserve about 80% of the Fresh Water, which is Trapped under the Mulching Rocks, which, alone will Eventually Pay for the Rocks — except that the Holy Angels do not Charge one another for any Mulching Rocks, nor for anything else: beCause they have what we call LOVE, which Shares the Natural Resources with everyone, whereby none are Excessively Rich, nor Extremely Poor; but, everyone is Moderately Rich, right here on the Good Old Earth, which can be Transformed into "The Environmentalists' Perfect Paradise!" (HOW almost Everyone can be Living in a Beautiful Manmade Paradise!) By The Worldwide People's Revolution!® Book 035C. Indeed, we can now put Capitalism into the Trash Can: beCause it is not Needed for True Prosperity. †§‡

03-05 [_] Well, my Friend, with a Good Plan like that, no one will have to Dream about going to Heaven when they Die: beCause they will just Naturally Want to be Born Again, right here, on the Good Old Earth, which has more than 50,000 Kinds of Sweet Juicy Fruits and Delicious Nuts to Choose from, not to Mention all of the Vegetables, Spices, and everything else to Eat. There are no less than a Trillion Different Dishes of Delicious Foods to Choose from! Moreover, if People Want to, they can make their own Granite Tables, and Cover them with Pure Gold, and Eat from their own Silver Plates, which, to me, are not nearly as Beautiful as Colorful Ceramic Dishes. †§‡

03-06 [_] O Good Pastor of Uncommon Sense, the Bible says that the Earth was Created for Mankind, and that the Heavens belong to the Gods, which makes Perfect Sense to me. After all, if Jehovah God had Wanted us to be Born Inside of Jupiter, that is where we would have been Born!

03-07 [_] Well, my Friend, Jesus said, *"Blest are the Meek, Teachable People: beCause they will Inherit the Good Earth, not Heaven: beCause the Earth was Made for the Righteous Ones." — The NMV of the Gospel According to Saint Bartholomew 10:27.* Therefore, that is most likely the Truth of it, which can be Proven in a Courtroom, if anyone is Interested in it. Most People are not Interested in it: beCause they HOPE to Escape from this Earth: beCause People have made it into a Living HELL, when they should have made it into a Wonderful Paradise for everyone! †§‡§§

03-08 [_] O Good Pastor of Uncommon Sense, are you Sure that this Earth was not also Created for Wicked People? Otherwise, WHY would there be so many Evil People in this World of Woes?

03-09 |_| Well, my Friend, in Reality, the Outside of the Earth is the Purgatory, where Sinners can be Tempted by Satan, and Tested for their Goodness, and Hopefully be Converted, whereby they might be Born on the Inside of the Earth during the Future: beCause that is the Paradise of God, which the Meek People will Inherit. ‡

03-10 [_] O Good Pastor of Uncommon Sense, have you ever Visited the Hollow Earth? Have you Seen the Paradise of God with your own Eyeballs? Or, do you get your Weird Beliefs from that Unholy Mutilated Bible, only?

— Chapter 04 —

Do all of the Animals Talk in the Kingdom of God?

04-01 [_] Well, the Short Answer is, YES, all of the large Animals Talk in the Kingdom of God, in whatever Languages that they are Tawt; but, their Nolij is very Limited: beCause most of them do not Like to Reed Bouks, even though they could Read Books, if they were Tawt how; but, they just Naturally have no Real Interest in it: beCause of being like many People, who do not Like to Reed Bouks: beCause they Prefer to Dream their Liivz away with Nonsense: beCause they were Born to be Servants, and not Masters, even as the Animals were also Born to be Servants, who are very Limited: beCause they do not have Hands to Work with in most Cases. However, a Horse or Ox can be very Useful, if they are Harnessed and Used Wisely: beCause they have a Lot of Strength, and can Drag Trees around, for Example. But, of what Great Value is a Bear? †§‡

04-02 [_] O Good Pastor of Uncommon Sense, a Bear is Good for putting the Fear of God into the Bones of Sinners, who are Cast Out of those **"GLORIOUS Swanky Hotels Castles and Fortresses!"** **(Beautiful Planned City States for WISE Intelligent Well-Educated People with Common Sense and Good Understanding!) By The Worldwide**

People's Revolution!® Book 019B, who must Learn their Lessons the Difficult Way: beCause of Rejecting Provable Truths. In Fact, they might have to be Eaten by those Mean Bears and Vicious Lions, just to Improve their Spirits. After all, what else are they Good for, except for Food for the Wolves? Indeed, Mankind can Liv Happily without any Criminals, except that they are Needed to Test the Spirits of the Righteous Ones, and perhaps Improve on them, a little at a Time, in this Life or during the next Life, which makes no Difference to God, just as long as we Eventually Learn our Lessons. †§‡§§

04-03 [_] Well, my Friend, most of the Animals were Created to be Symbolical. For Example, a Prostitute is Symbolized by a Stinking Skunk, who does her Work during the Darkness of Night, who Feasts on Dead Rotting Flesh, and does not Care how Filthy the Hole is, which she Crawls into; but, they are sometimes very Cute, and Cuddly. People generally Like them at a Distance. §‡

04-04 [_] The Bay Mule is used as an Ambulance, to Haul a Sick Person to the Doctor, as they did during the 1800s. Such a Mule can Pack 400 Pounds, for 6 Hours, or more, before getting too Tired: beCause they are Designed for Working. Of course, it is easier to Pack anything on Level Ground, than in Rocky Mountains with Slippery Trails. But, no Ambulance could get to the Victim in those Rocky Mountains, while the Mules might. Therefore, Mules and Horses are still being Used to Rescue People in Places that do not have Helicopters. Moreover, the Mules do not Object to it: beCause they generally like to be Obedient Servants, if they are not Overworked and Underfed. Good Masters should take Good

Care of their Work Animals, and Pray to God that they do not Speak Evil of their Masters during the Judgment Day, when nothing will be Secret. †§‡§§

04-05 [＿] O Good Pastor of Uncommon Sense, I am now Wondering just what the World would be Like, if Jesus Christ were Governing it? Would there be any Motorized Vehicles, at all? Would there be any Paved Highways? Any Airplanes? Any Army Tanks? What would it be Like?

04-06 [＿] Well, my Friend, I am Sure that there are Better Machines for Flying, than Airplanes and Noisy Dangerous Helicopters. They are called Flying Saucers: beCause of Looking like 2 Saucers that are put Together, with the one on Top being Upside Down. Ezekiel described them as a Wheel in the Midst of a Wheel. They fit Neatly into their Mother Ships, which are long Cigar-shaped Machines, which are not Affected by Gravity, which can Fly at 10,000 Miles per Hour with no Problems, up to 200,000 MpH, which are used to Transport People from one Planet to another one, if those Planets are Hollow. Not all of them are; but, most of them are, if they have Moons, which have their own Central Suns: beCause that is how God Designed them, which have Perfect Climates on the Insides of them, with Mountains, Rivers, Lakes, Forests, Fields, and all Kinds of Beautiful Animals: beCause there are no 2 Worlds that are just Alike: beCause each one is Unique, even as each of our Continents are Unique: beCause all of the Gods Love Diversity, whereby no 2 People Look just Alike, which is also True of the Aliens, who have their Similarities, also — such as 2 Eyes and 2 Ears, and also 2 Brains and 2 Testicles, which is Universal in Nature. †§‡
04-07 [＿] O Good Pastor of Uncommon Sense, what would be Required for the Animals to Speak English, for Example? Could God Open their Mouths, and make them Speak, like he did with Balaam's Ass in *Numbers 22,* which Sounds like a Jewish Fairy Tale?

04-08 [＿] Well, my Friend, it is no Fairy Tale: beCause Asses are very Intelligent Creatures, which you would Know, if you had been Raised with them and Horses, as I was. In Fact, we had a Horse that could Escape from almost any Pen that he was Locked up in: beCause he would use his Tongue to get Out. Therefore, we finally had to Wire the Gates Shut with Baling Wire, which he could not Untwist; but, he figured out how to Bite the Wire Off. So, we had to Invent a Way to Lock the Gates, which Inspired him to Kick one of the Gates Down when we went to Church, whereby he could get some Green Grass to Eat: beCause he was not at all Stupid. Therefore, after that, we just took him to the Green Pasture, and let him Eat for a couple Hours, and then put him back into his Pen, whereby he was Contented. He had a Tally Whacker that was at least 4 feet Long and 6-inches Wide at the Head of it, after Breeding a Mare, when he Withdrew it. It was quite a Sight to Behold, and he had about 20 Mares to Breed, which kept him Happy, which was a Springtime Family Royal Event, which Produced some Marvelous Babies, which Filled everyone with Wonder and Amazement! How could a Colt be Up and Running within only one Hour, and at Full Speed within a Month, when a Human Baby takes Months, just to Walk, and even Years to get up to Full Speed? †§‡

According to the Guinness World Records, Old Billy—rather appropriately named—is the **oldest horse** to have ever lived. Born in 1760, Old Billy lived to be a whopping 62 years of age.
Apr 24, 2020

ihearthorses.com › Fun Facts ▾
The Oldest Horses In History - iHeartHorses.com

Horse to Human Age Comparison Chart

Horse Age	Stage of Life	Human Age
27		78
30	Extreme Old Age	85.5
33		93
36		100.5

11 more rows • Sep 11, 2019

04-09 [_] O Good Pastor of Uncommon Sense, that would be like a Human Being Living for about 200 Years. It is interesting to note that Old Billy was kept Comfortable in a Barn with thick Stone Walls, which had a Consistent Temperature, and he was never Overworked, nor Overfed; but, he was Worked almost every Day, which Obviously Extended his Life. Moreover, he had Living Grasses to Eat, and no Cooked Foods. In Fact, he Lived in an Apple Orchard, and got Lots of Fallen Apples to Eat, which probably Explains his Old Age best of all. Therefore, People should Experiment with Feeding Horses and Cattle Fresh Fruits, just to Discover how Long that they might Liv. †§‡

Chimpanzees.

Sex	F
Birth date	c. 1937-1942
Death date	14 November 2017
Age	c. 77 to 83 years
Place of death or residence	United States, Lion Country Safari

An international team of paleontologists has discovered a well-preserved skeleton of a new tiny, tree-dwelling primate named **Archicebus achilles** that lived in what is now central China during Eocene about 55 million years ago. The find, described in the journal Nature, is the oldest known fossil primate skeleton. Jun 6, 2013

www.sci-news.com › paleontology › article01133-archice...
Oldest-Known Primate Fossil Found in China | Paleontology | Sci ...

04-10 [_] Well, my Friend, I would not Know all of the Details; but, I would Bet that Monkeys and Apes could easily Liv as Long as most People, if they were Properly Cared for.

— Chapter 05 —

Will there be any Capitalists in Heaven?

05-01 [_] So, I Asked Mr. Google, and this is the Response:

Is there Economics in heaven?

God is omnipotent, which means any resources needed (if any) can be instantly created. God and **Heaven** exist outside of the temporal universe, which means problems relating to future knowledge are eliminated. **There** are no **economic** problems in **Heaven**, and thus no need for an **economy**. Feb 12, 2018

force4good.me › 2018/02/12 › does-heaven-have-an-eco...
Does Heaven Have an Economy? | A Force for Good

05-02 [_] Imagine that — no Need for an Economy! It must be Based on the Presumption that People will not Need to EAT, Drink, Wear Clothing, nor Liv in Houses: beCause, their Imaginary "Heaven" will be Unearthly. Of course, there is nothing about such a Heaven within the *Holy Bible,* which barely Mentions Heaven, ànd never Explains anything about it, even though Jesus did Mention *the Kingdom of Heaven,* several Times, saying, for Example, that it was like 3 Barrels of Flour, which a Woman Leavened with Yeast, which Spread throughout the Dough, until it was all Leavened. (See *Matthew 13.*) It goes on to say, *"All of those Things Jesus Spoke to the Multitude in Parables; and without a Parable, he Spoke nothing to them: so that it might be Fulfilled, which was Spoken by the Prophet in Psalm 78, saying: 'I will open my Mouth in Parables; I will Utter Mysterious Things, which have been kept Secret from the Time of the Foundation of this World.' Then Jesus sent the Multitude away, and went into the House of his Host; and his Disciples came to him, saying: 'Declare to us the Meanings of the Parables, and especially the Meanings of the Tares in the Field.'"* So, he Explained it to them, saying: *"He who Sows the Good Seeds is the Son of a Holy Man; the Field is this World; the Good Seeds are Symbolical of the Children who were Born to Govern this World in the Holy Kingdom of All that is Good, which is the Government of God, which will eventually be Established on this Good Earth, during the Last Days; but, the Tares are the Unholy Children of the Wicked Ones, who were Born for Destruction; the Enemy who Sowed them is the Devil, who Seeks to Destroy all of Mankind; the Harvest is at the Time of the End of the Ages, and the Reapers are the Holy Angels, who will come with their Flying Spaceships, and Quickly*

47

Gather Out the Innocent Ones, to Save them Alive; but, the Evil Ones, who will not Obey my Commandments, shall be Burned with Unquenchable Fire, which will Reach to the Foundations of the Mountains, just to get Rid of their Abominations, and to Cleanse the Earth with Fire; and so shall it be during the End of this Worldly System of Things, when the Son of a Holy Man shall Send forth his Holy Angels, and they shall Gather Out of his Kingdom all Evil Things that Offend him, and them who do Iniquity; and they shall Cast them into a Furnace of Fire, you might say, where there shall be Weeping and Wailing and Gnashing of Teeths with Great Regrets: beCause of not Obeying the Man with the Spirit of Elijah, whom I will Send to Prepare the Way for my Second Coming, who will Reveal what is Required for all People to be Saved from their Sins; and then the Righteous Ones will Shine forth as the Brightness of the Sunstar in the Holy Kingdom of their Heavenly Father. Whosoever has Spiritual Ears that can Hear, let him Listen Carefully. Again, the Kingdom of Heaven is like a Treasure Trove that was Hidden in a Field during Ancient Times, which, when Found by a Poor Wise Man, he Covered it up with Dirt and Tree Leaves and Hid it Securely within the Volumes of his many Inspired Books; and then, for Great Joy over its Discovery, he goes and Sells all that he has, in order to Buy that Field, whereby he might Lawfully Obtain the Treasure in his own Field. Again, the Kingdom of Heaven is like a Merchant Man, who is Seeking Goodly Pearls of Great Truths; who, when he has Found one Special Pearl of Great Price, he goes out and Sells all that he has, in order to Buy that Pearl, for a Collector's Item: beCause he Realizes the Great Value of it, and how that nothing in this World of Wonders is more Precious than the Inspired Words of Provable Truths, which will one Day be Sold for a Great Price at an Auction Market, whereby that Wise Merchant Man will become Exceedingly Rich. Again, the Kingdom of Heaven is like a Net, which was Cast into the Sea, and Gathered all Kinds of Fishes, which, when it was Full, the Fishermen drew to Shore, and sat down with their Baskets, and Gathered the Good Fishes into their Vessels; but, they Cast the Bad Fishes back into the Sea. So shall it be at the End of the Ages — the Holy Angels shall come forth from Mount Zion, and Sever the Wicked Ones from among the Just Ones, and shall Cast those Wicked Ones into a Place that is like a Furnace of Fire, where there shall be Weeping and Wailing and Gnashing of Teeths with Great Regrets: beCause they shall See that only the Holy Ones will Enter into the Holy Kingdom of All that is Good, even if they are otherwise as Ignorant as Innocent Children, who Obey their Father and Mother: beCause it is the Right Thing to Do." And then Jesus Asked his Disciples if they Understood all of those Things? And they Assured him that they did. Therefore, he said to them, *"Therefore, every Scribe or Author, who is Instructed about the Kingdom that is coming from Heaven to this Earth, is like a Man who is an Householder, or Homeowner, who brings forth out of his Treasure Room Precious Things, both New and Old, which most People have not Seen before; or, have otherwise not taken Notice of them, who will now take Notice that all such Precious Things are of Equal Value, even if they are New and Strange to them."*

What is known as the bible of capitalism?

Adam Smith was an economist and philosopher who wrote what is considered the **"bible of capitalism,"** The Wealth of Nations, in which he details the first system of political economy. Oct 21, 2019

www.biography.com › scholar › adam-smith
Adam Smith - Wealth of Nations, Invisible Hand & Book - Biography

05-03 [ ] It appears that I am Forced to take the Time to Study "The Wealth of Nations," just to Understand how the Founding Fathers got Misled by a False Philosopher by the Name of Adam Smith, who must have been a Near Relative of Joseph Smith Junior, who got an entire Flock of Sheeps Led Astray, which turned out to be one of the Best Things that ever Happened! †§‡§§

Second, the **United States** does not have a strictly **capitalist** economy, but a mixed one. As such, it combines a high level of private ownership of capital and the means of production with relatively onerous regulation and taxation. Mar 1, 2016

www.cato.org › publications › commentary › bernie-not-s...
Bernie Is Not a Socialist and America Is Not Capitalist | Cato

05-04 [ ] It has Obviously never crossed the Minds of Capitalists, nor Socialists, that it is Possible for everyone to become Moderately RICH, and without Telling any Lies, nor Selling any Capitalist Trash! Indeed, I have already Explained it several Times, and in several Different Ways, for whomever might have Spiritual Ears that can Hear. Most People are simply Spiritually BLIND and DEAF, who cannot See the Light of Provable Truths, who will have to Suffer more and more, before they will come to their Riit Senses.

05-05 [_] There the Name of Adam Smith pops up again, as the Inventor of Capitalism. Surely he did not Wish it to become anything like what is Happening on Wall Street, nowadays; but, it has Evolved into a MONSTER with Intellectual Abscesses on the Brains of Deceived Capitalists, who have Created such a Complicated MESS, that not even they can Explain how it Works, which Depends on Confusion, rather than Reason and Logic, while Swangkeenomiks Depends Totally on Reason and Logic, and a Simple Lifestyle for everyone within those **"GLORIOUS Swanky Hotels Castles and Fortresses!" (Beautiful Planned City States for WISE Intelligent Well-Educated People with Common Sense and Good Understanding!) By The Worldwide People's Revolution!® Book 019B,** which will Belong to: **"The New RIGHTEOUS One-World Government!" (HOW to Establish a Righteous One-World Government without Going to WAR!) By The Worldwide People's Revolution!®** Book 056: beCause there is no Way on this Good Earth that anyone could Afford to BUY one! However, the Immortal Righteous One-World Government can easily Afford it: beCause it has the Power to Mint and Print New Money, even though Money is not Actually Needed for True Prosperity, as the Mayan Indians Proved, Centuries Ago, who did not Produce Criminals, Prisons, Taxes, Debts, Stocks, Bonds, nor any of that Trash.

05-06 |_| Just Stop and Think about that for a Time and half a Time. A Free-Market System allows Christians, Hindus, and Muslims the Freedom to Assist the less Fortunate People — such as the 6 Billion-plus People in this World of Woes, who do not have "Beautiful Swanky Stone Dome Home COMPLEXES!" (HOW to Build SECURE Tax-proof, Insurance-proof, Self-air-conditioned, Paint-proof, Rot-proof, Termite-proof, Mouse-proof, Fireproof, Tornado-proof, Hurricane-proof, Thief-proof, and BOMB-PROOF Houses!) By The Worldwide People's Revolution! Book 102, to Liv in, with Luscious All-Mineral Organic Gardens, Vineyards, and Orchards to Eat from, nor Home-craft Workshops with Well-made Swanky Tools to Work with, which Capitalism will never Furnish to them: beCause it is so Poor that it cannot even Provide Wholesome Natural Foods and Drinks for the Masses of Poor People to Consume, anywhere, who Liv with a Vain HOPE that some Glad Day they will Die and go to Heaven to be with Jesus; but, behold, it will never Happen: beCause that Myth was Invented by EDOMITES, who Wanted their Slaves to have such a Vain Hope, all of their Lives, while the Edomites are Exploiting them as their SLAVES of Various Kinds and Colors! In other Words, they had to come up with a Plan to Deceive all of those Poor Ignorant SLAVES, whereby they would not Want to go to WAR to Overthrow the Evil Empire, and get themselves Set Up Properly for LIVING! Indeed, the Edomites came up with the False OWNERSHIP Doctrine of the Devil, whereby everyone must OWN some Property, just to be a Citizen, and have a Right to VOTE: beCause all others are VAGABONDS and OUTCASTS! Yes, you can read it in the Fake Constitution, which would not even Permit Jesus Christ to VOTE: beCause he was not a Property Owner! Moreover, the Mayan Indians were able to show their Christian Charity to their Poor Naaberz, just as much as Modern Capitalist Christians: beCause they Fed and Clothed everyone among them, and Worked Together to Build Houses for everyone, whereby there were very few Poor People among them, who were only Poor if they were Crippled and/or Unable to Work; but, none of them went Hungry, if there was anything to Eat. Sometimes it did not Rain enough to Produce a Good Crop of anything. Therefore, beCause they did not have Large Cisterns for Water Storage, nor any Way to Preserve Foods in Canning Jars, they were at the Mercy of the Rain God, even as 99.99% of Americans are, right now, who are Relying on Helpless Farmers, who have no Large Cisterns for Water Storage. Indeed, Capitalism cannot Afford to Build any such Cisterns: beCause it is a False Economic System, which goes all of the Way Back to ADAM and EVE in the Garden of Eden Plan, when they were Cast Out of it, who did not Realize the IMPORTANCE of WATER! †§‡§§

Why is capitalism not good?   ⌃

Prominent among critiques of **capitalism** are accusations that **capitalism** is inherently exploitative, unsustainable and creates economic inequality, is anti-democratic and leads to an erosion of human rights while it incentivizes imperialist expansion and war.

en.wikipedia.org › wiki › Criticism_of_capitalism
Criticism of capitalism - Wikipedia

05-07 [_] Trust me, all of those Criticisms are Legitimate. Capitalism Exploits the Poor Ignorant Slaves to the Maximum, for the Sakes of a few Rich Hogs, who Liv like Donald Trump in their Big Mansions, and have their Weekend Parties with People like Jeffrey Epstein and Harvey Weinstein, who are just Naturally Produced by *"the Love of Money,"* which is *"the Root Cause for almost all Evils."* But, does it Bother the Consciences of any such Rich Hogs? NO! In Fact, if you Want to, you are Welcome to "get a good education, work hard, save your money, play by the rules, and exploit whomever you can." Indeed, many books have been written about it, which Explain HOW you can become another Capitalist and WINNER in their Satanic Game. Yes, they have all Kinds of Good Examples for you to Study — such as the Coke Companies, which Produce Flavored Drinks with Tons of Sugar to give to People Diabetes, whereby they become Real Winners, who get Addicted to all such Poisonous Drinks, Candies, Cookies, Cakes, Pies, Iced-creams, and whatever Satan and Sons and Dawterz can Produce for Sale — none of which is Fit to Eat nor Drink! †§‡§§

Is the US truly capitalist?

The **U.S.** is a mixed economy, exhibiting **capitalism** and socialism characteristics. Such a mixed economy embraces economic freedom when it comes to capital use, but it also allows for government intervention for the public good. Jul 9 2019

www.investopedia.com › ask › answers › united-states-co
Is the United States a Market Economy or a Mixed Economy?

05-08 [_] Without that Government Intervention, the Detroit River would probably still be on Fire from the Capitalist Chemicals that are Dumped into it, and Lake Erie would not have one Live Fish in it: beCause Capitalism has no Conscience, at all, being as Spiritually Dead as George Warmonger Bush and Little Dick Chicanery, Incorporated, who could care less how many of "those people over there" Die for their Oil, which Rightfully Belongs to Americans, who are "God's Chosen People," if you can Believe it, who can Do no WRong, just as long as they Repeatedly say: "God Bless America, and Protect our Troops!" But, what if God comes down from Jupiter, one of these Days, to Inspect Modern Sodom and Gomorrah, and Discovers that theses are NOT his Chosen People?

How does capitalism exploit the poor?

Capitalist exploitation thus consists in the forced appropriation by **capitalists** of the surplus value produced by workers. Workers under **capitalism** are compelled by their lack of ownership of the means of production to sell their labor power to **capitalists** for less than the full value of the goods they produce. Dec 20, 2001

plato.stanford.edu › entries › exploitation
Exploitation (Stanford Encyclopedia of Philosophy)

05-09 [_] In other Words, the Poor Work Slaves in Bangladesh, for Example, do not Own the Capitalist Stores that Sell the Rags that they Sew Together for less than Minimum Wages, who Earn about 2 Dollars per Day, and Work for 12 to 16 Hours, or else get Fired: beCause, there are 10,000 or more Unemployed Slaves waiting at the Gate of the Sewing Factory for a Capitalist Job with Poor Jobe, who is still Covered with Capitalist Boils, and does not know HOW to get Rid of them: beCause the Fake News Reporters never Explain it to them, nor DEMAND: "The GREAT Worldwide TELEVISED Court HEARING!" (That Great Meeting of the Most-Intelligent and Well-Educated Minds!) By The Worldwide People's Revolution!® Book 041B, whereby the Slaves might Learn the Whole Truth about those Lying Conniving Edomites. ‡

05-10 [_] Entropy means: Lack of Order, or Predictability; gradual Decline into Disorder. When People are not Set Up Properly on the Land for Living, they are at the Mercy of Chance, Luck, Superstition, Gambling Games, Crashing Stock Markets, Failing Businesses, and whatever Capitalism has to Offer to Ignorant Fools.

05-11 [_] How many Cars, Pickup Trucks, Cigarettes and Cokes could have been Sold without the Assistance of the Stock Market? Believe it or not, all People can Liv Healthy Happy Lives without any of those Evil Things, just by Living within Swanky Fortresses, where they use Elevators, Escalators and Electric Subway Trains, without any Accidents, Drunk Drivers, nor Traffic Tickets.

Democratic capitalism is neither the Kingdom of God nor without sin. Yet all other known systems of political economy are worse. Such hope as we have for alleviating poverty and for removing oppressive tyranny -perhaps our last, best hope - lies in this much despised system. A never-ending stream of immigrants and refugees seeks out this system.

05-12 [_] Those are Common Statements made by Capitalists, who never Tried the Swanky Fortress System, who never even Heard of "The New RIGHTEOUS One-World Government!" (HOW to Establish a Righteous One-World Government without Going to WAR!) By The Worldwide People's Revolution!® Book 056, who Imagine it to be a Satanic Government, if they do Hear about it: beCause that is what they have been Programmed to Believe; but, it is all just a Capitalist LIE: beCause such a System Assists everyone who is Willing and Able to Learn and Work, to become Moderately RICH, which Capitalism, Communism, and Socialism have Failed to Do, and in a BIG Way, which have Produced Extreme Poverty, whereby the Masses of People do not even have Fresh Clean Air to Breathe, Pure Living Water to Drink, nor Wholesome Natural Foods to Eat, much less, "Beautiful Swanky Stone Dome Home COMPLEXES!" (HOW to Build SECURE Tax-proof, Insurance-proof, Self-air-conditioned, Paint-proof, Rot-proof, Termite-proof, Mouse-proof, Fireproof, Tornado-proof, Hurricane-proof, Thief-proof, and BOMB-PROOF Houses!) By The Worldwide People's Revolution!® Book 102, to Liv in. Moreover, you do not need to Expect the Mainstream News Media to be Advertising any such Ideas at any Time soon: beCause they See those **"GLORIOUS Swanky Hotels Castles and Fortresses!" (Beautiful Planned City States for WISE Intelligent Well-Educated People with Common Sense and Good Understanding!) By The Worldwide People's Revolution!®** Book 019B, as a Great THREAT to their Evil Empire! ‡

— Chapter 06 —

Will People be Buying and Selling Things in Heaven?

06-01 [_] I Asked Mr. Google on the Internet; but, as Usual, he had no Idea. The Bible does not Mention it. Preachers Hesitate to Talk about it: beCause they Know that, *"No man has ascended up to heaven, except for the Son of man who came down from heaven ..."* even as it is Revealed in *John 3:13, King James Version (KJV),* slightly modified. Indeed, there is no Biblical Evidence that anyone ever went to Heaven; and "Heaven" is not even given a Definition, let alone, a Location. Here is what *Wikipedia* has to Offer for Information about Heaven:

Where is heaven located?

The area of the upper astral plane of Earth in the upper atmosphere where the various **heavens** are **located** is called Summerland (Theosophists believe hell is **located** in the lower astral plane of Earth which extends downward from the surface of the earth down to its center).

en.wikipedia.org › wiki › Heaven
Heaven - Wikipedia

How far up is heaven?

approximately 46 billion light years

Well, if you go by today's understanding of "the heavens" — meaning the totality of the universe outside Earth — they are approximately 46 billion light years higher. In fact, the heavens are so **high above** the Earth that human beings cannot possibly see everything in them. Sep 23, 2014

glassatmosphere.wordpress.com › 2014/09/23 › how-high...
How high are the heavens above the Earth? | The Glass Atmosphere

In Christianity, **heaven** is traditionally the location of the throne of God and the angels of God, and in most forms of Christianity it is the abode of the righteous dead in the afterlife.

en.wikipedia.org › wiki › Heaven_in_Christianity
Heaven in Christianity - Wikipedia

How many heavens are there?

In religious or mythological cosmology, the seven **heavens** refer to seven levels or divisions of **Heaven**. The concept, derived from ancient Mesopotamian religions, can be found in the Abrahamic religions such as Islam, Judaism and Christianity; a similar concept is also found in some Indian religions such as Hinduism.

en.wikipedia.org › wiki › Seven_Heavens
Seven Heavens - Wikipedia

Who will enter heaven?

In the King James Version of the Bible the text reads: Not every one that saith unto me, Lord, Lord, **shall. enter** into the kingdom of **heaven**; but he that doeth. the **will** of my Father which is in **heaven**.

en.wikipedia.org › wiki › Matthew_7 21
Matthew 7:21 - Wikipedia

06-02 [_] Wikipedia is so Ignorant that she does not know that "heaven" is NOT "the kingdom of heaven," even as Wisconsin Swiss Cheese is not Switzerland. The Kingdom of God, which is Coming to the Earth from Heaven, is a Heavenly Government, which has nothing to do with anyone going to Heaven, which is another Separate Subject. Wisconsin Swiss Cheese may be something like Swiss Cheese from Switzerland; but, it is not Switzerland, itself, nor Actual Swiss Cheese, at all, even if it looks like it: beCause, Authentic Swiss Cheese must come from Switzerland, and American Cheese must come from America, not from France, nor from Great Britain: beCause the Milk that makes the Cheese comes from America, only. The Government of God comes from Heaven, which is why it is called *"the Kingdom of Heaven,"* or, *"the Kingdom of God,"* which Originated in some Heavenly Place, which is never Identified within the *Holy Bible:* beCause, how could it have an Address, seeing that no one has ever Mapped Out the Endless Heavens, which go on and on for Billions of Trillions of Lightyears in all Directions!? Indeed, only the Most-High God knows the Beginning and the End of it, and he Knows that there are Countless Heavens and Earths; and only the Earths are Inhabited on the Insides and Outsides of them, while the Planets are Inhabited on the Insides, only. In Fact, Jehovah God Livz Inside of Jupiter, which has Concentric Worlds within Worlds, and he Livz in the very Center of all of those Concentric Worlds, where it is Safest for him to Liv. But, you do not have to Believe that to be Saved for another Life in this World: beCause this is the Purgatory, where Sinful People can be Purged from all of their Sins, if they Confess them and Forsake them, who may be Born on the Inside of this Earth, if they Overcome all of their Sins, and Stop Sinning. Otherwise, they will have to be Recycled, right here, wherever Jehovah God Chooses: beCause he is in Charge of all Earthly Souls, including our Pets and Livestock. Therefore, even if we Pass all of our Tests of Faith, Hope, Trust, Love, Patience, Persistence, and Obedience, we will not be going to Heaven; but, we can go to a Heavenly Place Inside of the Hollow Earth, by being Born there, even in: **"The Secret City of the Great King!" (HOW the True Church will Escape from the Great Tribulation!) By The Worldwide People's Revolution!® Book 042.**

Who is God and where is God?

In Christianity, the doctrine of the Trinity describes **God** as one **God** in three divine Persons (each of the three Persons is **God** himself). The Most Holy Trinity comprises **God** the Father, **God** the Son (Jesus), and **God** the Holy Spirit.

en.wikipedia.org › wiki › God

God - Wikipedia

06-03 [_] Notice that the Question was not Answered by Wikipedia; but, I will Answer it for them. God is the Supreme Ruler, and each World has a Supreme Ruler; and each Solar System has a Supreme Ruler, and each Galaxy has a Supreme Ruler, and each Universe has a Supreme Ruler, and there are Millions of Billions of them, which are Spaced Apart at Amazing Distances — all of which are "Experiment Stations," you might say: beCause the Gods are Experimenting with Various Kinds of Spirits and Bodies, which are called "Souls." Therefore, a Dog is a Soul, and you are also a Soul, who can and will Die, whereby your Spirit will be Separated from your Body: beCause, *the Soul that Sins shall Die,* which Means that the Spirit will Leave the Body, and God will Judge it, and Assign that Spirit to a New Body, if he Judges it to be Worthy of such a Body. Moreover, in almost all Cases, he Judges them to be Worthy to Liv Again, unless they have Blasphemed against the Holy Spirit, who is the Female Part of the Godhead, who Gently Leads us to our Heavenly Father, and Entices us to Seek All that is Good, which is God. Therefore, the Family of God, which consists of Billions of Trillions of Supreme Rulers, Livz in the Vast "Universe," which is not Measurable, even as the Stars are not Countable; but, you are Welcome to Try to Count them, if you Want to Drive yourself Insane! Moreover, just to show to you how Spooky it is to Sin, you must Remember that Jehovah / Yahweh God can Assign your Spirit to a Body that is Living Inside of Venus or Mars, whereby you can never See the Stars, much less, all of the Multitudes of Nebulas that have been "Seen" by Telescopes, which Reveal a Marvelous and Awesome World, which should Inspire anyone and everyone to Believe in a Great Creator God. ‡

06-04 [_] So, O Good Pastor of Uncommon Sense, are you Suggesting that we might Spend a Million or so Years Inside of Mars, as a Punishment for not Believing in a Great Creator God, after Seeing some of those Stars in the Sky? Would that be Perfectly Fair in the Eyes of God? †§‡

06-05 [_] Well, my Friend, I would say that it would be Appropriate for all Atheists, who Deny the Existence of a Great Creator God: beCause, without the Master Designer, how does one Obtain a Swiss Watch, for Example? How does one Create a Natural Law? Indeed, it is Nice to Discover all such Natural Laws; but, WHO Created them? Whomever it was, that Being is called GOD. But, as for WHO, or which God will Judge us, that is made Clear by the *Holy Bible,* whereby Jehovah God Appeared to Moses on Mount Sinai in all of his Naked Glory, as a Great GIANT of a MAN, who only did it to Show Moses how Small and Unimportant that he was, even as the Earth, Mars, Venus and Mercury are Insignificant Places, when Compared with Jupiter, Saturn, Uranus and Neptune.

The idea that a human soul belongs in **Heaven** and that **Earth** is merely a temporary abode in which the soul is tested to prove its worthiness became increasingly popular during the Hellenistic period (323 – 31 BC). Gradually, some Hebrews began to adopt the idea of **Heaven** as the eternal home of the righteous dead.

en.wikipedia.org › wiki › Heaven
Heaven - Wikipedia

What is the space between heaven and earth called?

Limbo, in Roman Catholic theology, the border place **between heaven** and hell where dwell those souls who, though not condemned to punishment, are deprived of the joy of eternal existence with God in **heaven**.

www.britannica.com › limbo-Roman-Catholic-theology
limbo | Definition & History | Britannica

It is inspired by the description of the New Jerusalem in Revelation 21:21: "The twelve **gates** were twelve pearls, each **gate** being made from a single pearl." ... Those not fit to enter **heaven** are denied entrance at the **gates**, and descend into Hell.

en.wikipedia.org › wiki › Pearly_gates
Pearly gates - Wikipedia

What are the three levels of heaven?

According to this vision, all people will be resurrected and, at the Final Judgment, will be assigned to one of **three** degrees of glory, called the celestial, terrestrial, and telestial kingdoms.

en.wikipedia.org › wiki › Degrees_of_glory
Degrees of glory - Wikipedia

Who will not get into the kingdom of heaven?

9Do you **not** know that the unrighteous[1] **will not** inherit the **kingdom of God**? **Do not** be deceived: neither the sexually immoral, nor idolaters, nor adulterers, nor men who practice homosexuality,[2] 10nor thieves, nor the greedy, nor drunkards, nor revilers, nor swindlers **will** inherit the **kingdom of God**.

www2.bc.edu › james-bretzke
1 Corinthians 6:9-10: The Original Greek Various English Translations

What is the 1st heaven?

The first **heaven** is described as being made of water and is the home of Adam and Eve, as well as the angels of each star.

en.wikipedia.org › wiki › Seven_Heavens
Seven Heavens - Wikipedia

What does Bible say about 3 heavens?

A third concept of **Heaven**, also called shamayi h'shamayim (שמי השמים or "**Heaven** of **Heavens**"), is mentioned in such passages as Genesis 28:12, Deuteronomy 10:14 and 1 Kings 8:27 as a distinctly spiritual realm containing (or being traveled by) angels and **God**.

en.wikipedia.org › wiki › Third_Heaven
Third Heaven - Wikipedia

What is the three levels of heaven?

The celestial kingdom is the highest of the **three** degrees of glory. It is thought by the LDS Church to be the "third **heaven**" referred to by the apostle Paul in the King James Version of 2 Corinthians 12:2 and it is said to correspond to the "celestial bodies" and "glory of the sun" mentioned in 1 Corinthians 15:40–41.

en.wikipedia.org › wiki › Degrees_of_glory
Degrees of glory - Wikipedia

Who is going to heaven according to the Bible?

In the Book of Acts, the resurrected Jesus ascends to **heaven** where, as the Nicene Creed states, he now sits at the right hand of God and will return to earth in the Second Coming.

en.wikipedia.org › wiki › Heaven_in_Christianity

Heaven in Christianity - Wikipedia

Do our dogs go to heaven?

Pop's dream of dead **dogs** as angelic beings and Mol's reference to "**dog heaven**" suggest there is belief that like their human counterparts, **dogs** also **go to heaven** and become angels as a reward for their good conduct on earth. In many cultures and religions **dogs** are more than protection and security. May 29, 2017

theconversation.com › all-dogs-go-to-heaven-78272

All dogs go to heaven - The Conversation

Rev 22:15   **For without are** dogs, and sorcerers, and whoremongers, and murderers, and idolaters, and whosoever loveth and maketh a lie.

Which country is heaven on earth?

Switzerland

Switzerland, also known as **heaven on earth**. Mar 1, 2004

www.theguardian.com › mar › population.hughmuir

Switzerland, also known as heaven on earth - The Guardian

What is God's age?

I'd even say there was no **God** before the end of the Neolithic **age**, and that means **God** is roughly 7,000 years old. Aug 30, 2011

www.theguardian.com › aug › how-old-is-god-queries

Notes and queries: God's age? Somewhere between 39 and

How long is purgatory?

Regarding the time which **purgatory** lasts, the accepted opinion of R. Akiba is twelve months; according to R.

en.wikipedia.org › wiki › Purgatory

Purgatory - Wikipedia

How hard is it for a rich man to enter heaven?

"The eye of a needle" is scripture quoting Jesus recorded in the synoptic gospels: I tell you the truth, it is hard for a rich man to enter the kingdom of heaven. Again I tell you, it is easier for a **camel** to go through the eye of a needle than for a rich man to enter the kingdom of God.

en.wikipedia.org › wiki › Eye_of_a_needle
Eye of a needle - Wikipedia

06-06 [_] Notice that Jesus said nothing about anyone entering into Heaven; but, only into the KINGDOM or GOVERNMENT of GOD. However, Extremely Ignorant People ASSUME that he was talking about People going to Heaven, when he was NOT. They get the Idea from a Perverted Song, called: ♫ *"When we All Get to Heaven!"* and other Misleading Songs, called HYMNS, which are not *Biblical.* In Fact, a lot of False Beliefs are Derived from Satanic Songs: beCause Satan uses those Songs to Pervert our Minds, and get us to Believe his Lies: beCause those Songs are CHANTS, which often Repeat the same Lies, over and OVER! Therefore, if you Sing a Lie, over and over, long enough, and LOUD Enough, you are Bound to Believe that it is the Truth. For Example, many Americans Sing: ♫ *"I'm so Proud to be an American, where at least I Know that I am Free to Pay all of my Endless Bills, and Consume all of my Countless Pills!"* Yes, they Chant a Similar Song at every Trump Political Rally: beCause they Hope that you will Believe it, also, and Sing along. †§‡§§

What is our reward in heaven?

Rejoice, and be exceedingly glad, for great is. **your reward in heaven.** For that is how they. persecuted the prophets who were before you.

en.wikipedia.org › wiki › Matthew_5:12
Matthew 5:12 - Wikipedia

God **will** give us **new bodies in heaven -- bodies** that **will** be similar to Christ's **body** after His resurrection. The Bible says that Christ, "by the power that enables him to bring everything under his control, **will** transform our lowly **bodies** so that they **will** be like his glorious **body"** (Philippians 3:21). Oct 2, 2005

www.seattlepi.com › news › article › We-will-be-given-ne...
We will be given new bodies in heaven - seattlepi.com

06-07 [_] First of all, they Ask the Question, "Will we be given New Bodies in Heaven?" and then they take Words Out of Context, and make it out that we will be in Heaven when we get New Bodies; but, Paul said nothing about being in Heaven. So, what about our Great Reward in

Heaven? Well, it is a Mistranslation, which should read: *Blest are you, when Evil Men shall Revile against you, and Persecute you, and shall say all Kinds of Evil Things against you, Falsely, for my Name's Sake. Rejoice, and be Exceedingly Glad: beCause Great shall be your Reward in the Kingdom that is Coming from Heaven to the Earth: beCause, so did they Persecute the Prophets, who came before you, and who will come after you, who will Enter into that Holy Kingdom, which is Prepared for those Wise People who Love All that is Good, which is God. Therefore, Pray to God that his Holy Kingdom will Come to this Earth, and that his Will will be Done on this Earth, even as it is now Done in Heavenly Places, which will come to pass during the Last Days, when all of the Nations will be Governed by the Children of Israel, from "The Great World TEMPLE of PEACE!" (The Glory of Jerusalem Arises Again in the Great State of Flexible Texas!) By The Worldwide People's Revolution!®* Book 017B.

06-08 [_] O Good Pastor of Uncommon Sense, that is not how the Bible reads. You are Adding Lies to the Word of God. You are putting yourself in Danger of Hellfire! Therefore, Edit it OUT!‡

06-09 [_] Well, my Friend, you must Remember that the Holy Spirit did not Die; and those are the Words that she Gave to me to Write. Therefore, they are Written, and I will not Change them: beCause you did not Point Out any Lies in them. Indeed, just Exactly which Words are Lies? †§‡

06-10 [_] O Good Pastor of Uncommon Sense, it only makes Sense that our Great Reward is in Heaven: beCause God has Created a Special World for each one of us who Believe and Obey him.

— **Chapter 07** —

What Kind of Music will People Listen to in Heaven?

07-01 [_] Mr. Google does not venture to say anything about it, lest someone might be Offended, if their Favorite Music was not Played in Heaven. However, when you Discover that this Good Earth is our one and only "Heaven and Hell," you Realize that it is up to us to make our own Music, and our own Heaven or Hell: beCause we have the Power to Do that. Therefore, we should be Happy with whatever we have made for ourselves. Personally, I do not care to Listen to most Music: beCause it is just NOISE in my Ears; but, I do Enjoy Classical Music, and some Hymns. ‡

07-02 [_] O Good Pastor of Uncommon Sense, some Silly People Sincerely Believe that they will have nothing to Do when they get to Heaven — as in, no more Work to Do — no Gardening, no Harvesting of Fruits, no Cooking, no Clothes to Wash, and no Houses to Clean: beCause Holy Angels will be doing it all for them! Where they get such Ideas from is a Total Mystery, since there is nothing within the *Holy Bible* about it. Perhaps they are just Dreaming?

07-03 [_] Well, my Friend, those Dreams that People have can most likely Account for many of their Beliefs. For Example, there was a Caveman, who Lived about 60,000 Years Ago, who Dreamed about Driving a Modern Car of a Freeway Overpass, in spite of never Seeing a Car, nor a Highway. Therefore, when he told his Wife what he saw in his Dream, she said: "Honey, I had that same Kind of a Spooky Dream, that we were riding in a Car, and it ran Out of Gas, and would not Start; and then a Camel came along, and Offered to us a Ride. Therefore, we got onto the Camel, which was suddenly about 40 feet Tall and much larger than a Normal Camel, which Frightened me to Death; but, then I Woke Up in a Zoo with a Bunch of Monkeys, who were Eating Tin Cans." And he said, "Sweetheart, I have no Idea what you have been Eating; but, I suggest that you Change your Diet: beCause you are having Bad Dreams." And she said, "Who is it that puts those Dreams into our Heads?" And he said, "What makes you Think that someone is Managing our Dreams?" And she said, "There is no Way that we could Dream about Things that we have never Seen." And he said, "But, suppose that we Lived in other Worlds, where we did get to See all such

Things, which Stuck in our Memories?" And she said, "I suppose that it is Possible. However, I have Dreamed about Things that Happened to me, Years Later, long after having the Dreams." And he said, "Well, that is Proof that there is some God, who Knows what will Happen to us during the Future, who gives to us all such Dreams." And she said, "That is Utterly Ridiculous: beCause there are Millions of People, who are Dreaming every Night, while they are Sleeping. Therefore, how could any God Manage the Dreams of every Person in the World, and also in all of those other Countless Worlds? It would be too much for one Old God to Manage." And he said, "Well, maybe each Person has a Guardian Angel, who Manages their Dreams?" And she said, "I suppose that such a Thing could be Possible; but, how would that Guardian Angel get into our Heads?" And he said, "Perhaps through our Eyes, Ears, Noses, or Mouths." †§‡§§

07-04 [_] O Good Pastor of Uncommon Sense, everyone Knows that you just made up that little Story, yourself, which never Actually Happened. Therefore, it is not *Scriptural.*

07-05 [_] Well, my Friend, in order to make it *Scriptural,* all that we have to Do is to Remove the 60,000-year-old Caveman, and put the Story into the *Holy Bible,* and X-number of People will Believe it from then onward. After all, have you not had Dreams like that, yourself? †§‡

07-06 [_] Yes, of course, we have all had Silly Dreams that we could not Explain; but, that does not Mean that they came from some Imaginary God, nor even from one of his Holy Angels. †§‡§§

07-07 [_] Well, they had to Come from Somewhere: beCause there is no Way that a Dream could Invent itself, is there? Indeed, that would be like your Head Inventing itself! No way! It could never Happen in a Billion Years!

07-08 [_] O Good Pastor of Uncommon Sense, it seems to me that our Bodies and Minds are far too Complicated for anyone but God to Explain; and, the only Reason that he could Explain it, is beCause of Creating it that Way. †§‡

07-09 [_] Well, my Friend, when you Think about it, it is not Difficult to Believe in a Great Creator God: beCause he has Arranged it all that Way, whereby there is only ONE Rational Conclusion, which is the Fact that there must be a Great Creator God, whose Ways are Far Passed our Good Understanding, which would be like a Chair Understanding how the

Table was Made, having no Eyes, Ears, Nostrils, nor Brains for Understanding anything, being Spiritually Dead, you might say.

07-10 [_] O Good Pastor of Uncommon Sense, it Looks like we Human Beings will just have to Accept the Fact that we were Created by some Marvelous God, who may easily Appear in the Dark Awesome Rolling Clouds of a FEARSOME SKY, along with tens of thousands of his Holy Angels, at some Time during the Future, and take us by Surprise, like a Tiger in the Forest! †§‡

— Chapter 08 —

Will People be Smoking Marijuana in Heaven?

08-01 [_] O Good Pastor of Uncommon Sense, if there is no Marijuana in Heaven to get High on, I do not care to go there.

08-02 [_] Well, my Friend, the "Heaven" that People Vainly Imagine themselves going to, is right here on the Good Old Earth, which we can make into a Heavenly Place to Liv. Therefore, if you Want to Smoke Marijuana, just Check the Appropriate Boxes in: "The Complete SURVEYS of our VALUES!" (SURVEYS of Religious Spiritual Political Governmental Sexual Social Moral Economical Business Labor Habitual and Miscellaneous VALUES!) By The Worldwide People's Revolution!® Book 059, and you can have whatever you Want, Free of all Charges: beCause God has Provided all Things, Free of all Charges. But, of course, you might have to take 15 Minutes to Plant some Seeds in the Ground, in the Holes between those "Profitable Swanky MULCHING ROCKS!" (30 Advantages for Using Swanky Mulching Rocks in an All-Mineral Organic Garden!) By The Worldwide People's Revolution!® Book 098.

08-03 [_] Those are just some of the 624 Swanky Mulching Rocks that our Selected King got from South Dakota, called "Crazyhorse Granite," which is the Second-most Dense Granite in the United States of America. The Densest Granite is found in Vermont, which is Black. You can See that this Granite is much more Beautiful, and a bit Cooler; but, not nearly as Cool as White Granite. ‡

08-04 [_] O Good Pastor of Uncommon Sense, we could Plant a Marijuana Seed in each of those Holes, in every other Row in the Garden, and Grow as many as 2,500 Plants in just one Acre, Times 2,000 Dollars per Plant, would equal about 5 Million Dollars; or, enough Money to Buy 16,666 Mulching Rocks the next Year, for Planting 1.6 Acres; and then, from then on, we would only have to Attend to 2 Acres of Marijuana Plants, to have a Yearly Income of 10 Million Dollars, which would soon Pay for the Construction of one of those: "Beautiful Swanky Stone Dome Home COMPLEXES!" (HOW to Build SECURE Tax-proof, Insurance-proof, Self-air-conditioned, Paint-proof, Rot-proof, Termite-proof, Mouse-proof, Fireproof, Tornado-proof, Hurricane-proof, Thief-proof, and BOMB-PROOF Houses!) By The Worldwide People's Revolution!® Book 102, which would be Worth a Billion Dollars! Indeed, a thousand Voluntary Working Soldiers could get Together and Build one of those "GLORIOUS Swanky

Hotels Castles and Fortresses!" (Beautiful Planned City States for WISE Intelligent Well-Educated People with Common Sense and Good Understanding!) By The Worldwide People's Revolution!® Book 019B, which the Federal Government would Naturally Discover in their Spy Satellite in the Sky, and Tax us for it. However, if we first of all Established "The New RIGHTEOUS One-World Government!" (HOW to Establish a Righteous One-World Government without Going to WAR!) By The Worldwide People's Revolution!® Book 056, there would be ZERO Taxes; and therefore, we could Really Prosper, like no other People ever Prospered before: beCause of having a Yearly Income of 10 Billion Dollars, from only 1,000 Acres of Marijuana Plants: beCause of Harvesting 10,000,000 Dollars from just one Acre, from 5,000 Plants — not to Mention the Equal Number of many Beautiful Flowers that we could Grow in the Rows between the Marijuana Plants, Legally, with the Permission of that Good Government! †§‡

08-05 [_] Well, my Friend, with a Yearly Income of 10 Billion Dollars, it would not be long before you would all become Moderately RICH, without Telling any Lies, nor Selling any Capitalist Trash. Yes, you could Accomplish it with Free Enterprise, alone. But, of course, you would have to "VOTE for The GOAT!" (The New Political Party that has Guaranteed Solutions for our Massive Problems!) By The Worldwide People's Revolution!® Book 109, come next November, instead of Voting for some Dimwitcrat or Reprobate! ‡

08-06 [_] O Good Pastor of Uncommon Sense, why not Plant 10,000 Acres, and have a Yearly Income of 100 Billion Dollars, whereby we might Afford to Build no less than 1,000 of those "Beautiful Swanky Stone Dome Home COMPLEXES!" (HOW to Build SECURE Tax-proof, Insurance-proof, Self-air-conditioned, Paint-proof, Rot-proof, Termite-proof, Mouse-proof, Fireproof, Tornado-proof, Hurricane-proof, Thief-proof, and BOMB-PROOF Houses!) By The Worldwide People's Revolution!® Book 102, each Year: beCause of having Voluntary Labor? Indeed, I will Cheerfully Volunteer to do the Gardening for the next 10 Years, until my Swanky Stone Dome Home Complex gets Built. †§‡

08-07 [_] Well, my Friend, if all of the Labor is Voluntary, such Wise People could Afford to Buy the Materials for Building no less than 10,000 of those Stone Dome Home Complexes per Year, with an Annual Income of 10 Billion Dollars: beCause, 10 Million Dollars will easily Buy all of the Tools and Building Materials for 100 Houses; and then, when all of those Houses are Finished, you can Write out Deeds for each Voluntary Working Soldier, who can then be the Proud Owners of their Swanky Stone Dome Home COMPLEXES! — Thanks to those Marijuana Plants, and a little Playing in the Garden! †§‡

08-08 [_] O Good Pastor of Uncommon Sense, why not Grow 100,000 Acres of Marijuana Plants, and use the Rows in between them for Growing Foods to Eat, instead of Flowers, whereby 100,000 People could become Moderately RICH: beCause of Building no less than 100,000 Houses per Year, while the Marijuana is Growing, which would Amount to 1,000,000 Houses within only 10 Years; and all of those Houses would be Worth no less than 10 Trillion Dollars on Today's Market? Indeed, it is possible for one Person to take Good Care of only one Acre of Plants: beCause of not having to Weed nor Water them: beCause the "Profitable Swanky MULCHING ROCKS!" (30 Advantages for Using Swanky Mulching Rocks in an All-Mineral Organic Garden!) By The Worldwide People's Revolution!® Book 098, and a Proper Watering System takes care of that.‡

08-09 [_] Well, my Friend, with a Proper Garden, you might easily Grow 3 Trillion-dollars-worth of Plants on 100,000 Acres, which is only 160 square Miles of Land, counting Roads, which is less than 13 Miles Square; or, 13 by 13, which is just a Fraction of "A New Jerusalem in the Great State of Flexible Texas!" (HOW to make Good Use of the Mississippi River!) By The Worldwide People's Revolution!® Book 090, which will be about 100 Miles by 100 Miles, if the Good People of Texas go along with the Plan, which they should. After all, almost everyone in Texas would Prefer to Liv in a 10-million-dollar Swanky Stone Dome Home COMPLEX, as Opposed to Living in their Wooden / Plastic Firetrap Mouse-infested Cockroach Dens! †§‡§§

08-10 [_] O Good Pastor of Uncommon Sense, it all Sounds like a Workable Plan, until you Consider those Lying Conniving Edomites, who are Bound to figure out HOW to Tax such People Out of Business, unless they Form their own City State, and Manage themselves, Properly. †§‡§§

— Chapter 09 —

Will Heaven be in TEXAS?

09-01 [_] Why have Heaven in Texas, when it could be everywhere, just by Establishing: "The New RIGHTEOUS One-World Government!" (HOW to Establish a Righteous One-World Government without Going to WAR!) By The Worldwide People's Revolution!® Book 056?

09-02 [_] O Good Pastor of Uncommon Sense, do you not Realize that most People are not Worthy of a Heavenly Place to Liv? For Example, most of them are Greedy, Selfish Hogs and Barking Dogs, as God might say, which can be Proven at any Grocery Store, where those Hogs are Lined Up with their Grocery Carts, which are Full of Dog Foods and Hog Slop: beCause they have no Idea what is Good for them, nor what is Bad for them, who often Weigh twice as much as they should for their own Good Health, who Suffer with Various Pains, Sicknesses and Diseases. †§‡§§

09-03 [_] Well, my Friend, I do not know about "most" People; but, for Sure, a certain Percentage of People are Unworthy of any Heavenly Places to Liv, and they could all be Born in Slums, in Africa, India, Brazil, or in Lost Angels, Californicate; but, not in Kentucky, Tennessee, Indiana, Vermont, Wisconsin, Montana, Idaho, Wyoming, Utah, nor in any other Beautiful Places — such as Europe, which has Produced some of the Finest Human Beings in the World, most of whom are Well-Disciplined, Honest, Trustworthy, Courteous, Kind, Generous, Loving, Respectful People, who Deserve to Liv in those "Beautiful Swanky PALACES!" (A New Concept in Living Habits — Swanky Palaces for Poor People!) By The Worldwide People's Revolution!® Book 066. ‡

09-04 [_] O Good Pastor of Uncommon Sense, each Person can be his own Judge, and Choose where to Liv, and with whom, just by Filling Out and Filing: "The Complete SURVEYS of our VALUES!" (SURVEYS of Religious Spiritual Political Governmental Sexual Social Moral Economical Business Labor Habitual and Miscellaneous VALUES!) By The Worldwide People's Revolution!® Book 059. Moreover, if they are too Lazy to Do that, they can Fill Out and File: "The Simplistic SURVEYS of our VALUES!" Book 059B, which has a Beautiful Free Book Preview on Amazon, which everyone should Reed, after getting lots of Sleep. ‡

09-05 [_] Well, my Friend, most Americans have caught up on their Sleep, after being Quarantined in their Houses. However, instead of Fasting and Praying, they have been Eating and Drinking, which did not Profit them anything. Therefore, what is God going to Do to Help them? Maybe they should Study: "What will you Do when the Rain STOPS?" (God's Last Resort to Save Mankind from his MADNESS!) By The Worldwide People's Revolution!® Book 101!

09-06 [_] O Good Pastor of Uncommon Sense, I Realize that you Want to Help People, who Desperately Need some Help; but, they have no Interest in Helping themselves. Therefore, they are Lost Souls. Therefore, you might as well Forget about Helping them. After all, they Hope to Die and go to Heaven. †§‡

09-07 [_] Well, my Friend, what you say is True: beCause most of them do not even Want to Reed Goud Bouks; and, if they do read a book, they only look for Faults: beCause they are Negative-minded. Therefore, it will Require some Great Famine to get them Inspired. Indeed, their Bellybuttons might have to be Rubbing on their Backbones for Hunger and Thirst, before they will come to their Right Senses with *the Prodigal Son of Luke 15.*

09-08 [_] O Compassionate Pastor of Uncommon Good Sense, the Reverend Billy Graham Wasted some 60 Years of his Life, in a Vain Effort to Lead the Masses of People to Christ, and it Looks like they all Chose to go in the Opposite Direction, except for a Handful like you, who got Lost in the Darkness of Ignorance: beCause of not having an Understandable Bible to read. Indeed, they never Discovered "The New MAGNIFIED Version of the Book of REVELATION!" (The Understandable Version of the Most-Controversial Book in the Whole World!) By The Worldwide People's Revolution!® Book 105, much less: "The New MAGNIFIED Version of The GOOD NEWS According to Saint LUKE!" (The Magnified Gospel of Saint Luke in Plain English!) By The Worldwide People's Revolution!® Book 061, and: "The New MAGNIFIED Version of the Book of ACTS!" (The Understandable Version of the Acts of the Apostles in Plain English!) By The Worldwide People's Revolution!® Book 063, which Reveals what the First Church of Jesus Christ did, which brought upon them Great Persecutions.‡

09-09 [_] Well, my Friend, beCause of that Persecution, they were no doubt Better People; but, it did not last very long, before they "went to Hell," anyway: beCause of not having a Clear, Readable nor Understandable Bible. Therefore, whom should we Blame for the Spiritual Disaster that we now have? {See: "Was Billy Graham Greatly Deceived?" (Giving Honor to whom Honor is Due!) By The Worldwide People's Revolution!® Book 083.}

09-10 [_] O Good Pastor of Uncommon Sense, if I am reading my Bible Correctly, everything is going according to God's Master Plan, and only a Handful of People will be Saved from the Wrath to Come. Yes, as it was during the Days of Noah, so shall it be during the Last Days, when most of the People will be Eating and Drinking, Marrying and giving in Marriage, Building Houses, and Doing whatever People Do, when Suddenly the Fire of God will come down and Destroy all of them! And then, God will begin all over again to Inhabit the Earth with Righteous People. †§‡§§

— Chapter 10 —

The Happy Conclusion!

10-01 [_] So, this is what a Verse in the *Psalms* states:

Psa 115:16 **The heaven,** *even the heavens,* *are* **the** LORD'S: but **the** earth hath he given to **the** children of men.

10-02 [_] Therefore, why would anyone Imagine that he is going to Heaven when he Dies?

10-03 [_] O Good Pastor of Uncommon Sense, it is a Dreadful Thot, to Think that we might be Born here again, into this Hateful World, whereby we are nothing but SLAVES of the Evil Empire.

10-04 [_] Well, my Friend, the Good News is this: We, the People, can Change all of that, and Liberate ourselves from the Evil Empire, just by Campaigning and Voting for: "The New RIGHTEOUS One-World Government!" (HOW to Establish a Righteous One-World Government without Going to WAR!) By The Worldwide People's Revolution!® Book 056. However, a Woman on Facebook told me that she already knows what the Bible says about such a BAD Government, and she Wants nothing to do with it. However, I told her that the *Holy Bible* has Wonderful Things to say about the New Righteous One-World Government, which will be Governed by the KING of Kings! Therefore, she should Study the Books that are Written by the Man with the Spirit of Elijah, who has Come to Prepare the Way for the Second Coming of Jesus Christ; but, did I Hear from her again? NO! Indeed, she was a "Christian" in Name, only, who had no Interest in making this a Good World for everyone to Liv in. Therefore, she just Guaranteed herself a Place in the Unholy Kingdom of Satan, the Devil, who also has no Interest in making this a Good World for everyone to Liv in. In Fact, he is her Master, and the Master Slave Driver of everyone who Opposes "The CONSTITUTION for the New RIGHTEOUS One-World Government!" (HOW all Peoples can get True Justice, and Celebrate the Great Year of JUBILEE!) By The Worldwide People's Revolution!® Book 016B. ‡

10-05 [_] O Good Pastor of Uncommon Sense, there are no Greater Deceptions in this World of Woes, than those that are Tawt by "The Hopeless Church of Little Faith!" (The Unholy Church of Graceful

Sinners, who are Mostly just Liars and Hypocrites!) **By** The Good Pastor of Uncommon Sense! Book 121. Therefore, you must now Burden yourself by Writing that Inspired Book, with the Hope that someone might Study it, even though it is Doubtful: beCause almost everyone Belongs to that Unholy Church of Graceful Sinners, who are Mostly just Liars and Hypocrites! After all, they Draw Near to God with their Mouths; but, their Hearts are Far from him, just as it is Written in *Isaiah 29:13; Matthew 15:8; Mark 7:6; and Jeremiah 12:2.* Indeed, they are a Lost and Confused Generation of Deceived People, who Vainly Imagine that they are going to Heaven, to Pollute it with their Capitalist Trash, who do not Want to Pick Fruits from Trees: beCause that might Require a little Work; but, they do not Know that a Healthy Person does not Object to Work: beCause it makes him Feel GOOD! ‡

10-06 [_] Well, my Friend, such a Person would first of all have to Humble himself by Fasting and Confessing his Dietary Sins, whereby he might be Physiologically Born Again, as Jesus was trying to Explain to Nicodemus in *John 3;* but, behold, Nicodemus could not Understand him, and did not get to reed: "The New MAGNIFIED Version of The GOOD NEWS According to Saint JOHN!" (The Gospel According to Saint John Zebedee Boanerges [pronounced Boo-an-er-jeez] in Plain English!) By The Worldwide People's Revolution!® Book 062, which Explains Exactly what it Means to be Born Again, which anyone can Prove for himself, just by Following: "The Proper RULES for FASTING!" (The Complete Instruction Manual for True Repentance!) By The Worldwide People's Revolution!® Book 046, which is a Companion Book of: "HOW to Become a HOLY Man!" (40 Good Reasons WHY People Should FAST and PRAY!) By The Worldwide People's Revolution!® Book 045, which is a Companion Book of all of the other Inspired Books that are Listed in Chapter 40, which any Congregation of 100 or more People can Buy and put into their Church Truth-brary, whereby they can all get to Study them, Carefully, and then, after everyone has "red" them, they can Discuss them with Clear Minds: beCause of Obeying "The Gospel According to our Elected King!" (The Good News from the Most Modern Perspective!) By The Worldwide People's Revolution!® Book 077.

10-07 [_] O Good Pastor of Uncommon Sense, that would Require Diligence and Persistence, just for any Church to "reed" all of those Inspired Books; but, I would not say that it is an Impossible Thing for them to Do: beCause, you have "red" all of those Exceptionally Good Books several Times, and you are still not Sick of them! Therefore, if you could Do it, so can they. †§‡

10-08 [_] Well, my Friend, there is a Great Reward Patiently Waiting for whomever Reedz and Oobaaz those Good Books: beCause they will get to Liv in Mount Zion during the Great Tribulation: beCause of Flying Away on the Wings of a Great Eagle! Yes, it is Revealed in: **"The Secret City of the Great King!" (HOW the True Church will Escape from the Great Tribulation!) By The Worldwide People's Revolution!®** Book 042. Therefore, if anyone is Interested in Escaping from the Great Tribulation, they should Study that Inspired Book, which is a Companion Book of several other Inspired Books: beCause, it is not Safe to put too much Important Information into just one Book, lest Satan should Discover it, and Try to Destroy it. †§‡

10-09 [_] O Good Pastor of Uncommon Sense, most People will not Accept what you Teach with any Seriousness: beCause of Assuming that you are just another Fool: beCause they do not Know WHO you are, nor WHY you have Written any Books, at all: beCause they are Unfamiliar with the *Scriptures,* and especially with the *Old Testament.* Therefore, they will have to Suffer through the Great Tribulation, just to Refine their Minds, and to Purify their Thinking Apparatuses. †§‡§§

10-10 [_] Well, my Friend, no one can Rightfully say that I did not Do my Best to WARN them about the Dangers of being Extremely Ignorant. Therefore, they will Fulfill that *Scripture,* which says: *My People Perish for a Lack of Trq Nolij ... — NMV of Hosea 4:6.*

Hos 4:6   My people are destroyed for **lack of knowledge**: because thou hast rejected **knowledge**, I will also reject thee, that thou shalt be no priest to me: seeing thou hast forgotten the law **of** thy God, I will also forget thy children.

— Chapter 40 —

A Long List of other Fascinating Literature by the same Inspired Author

[ ] 40-001 — "LIGHTNING **Versus the** Lightning Bug!" (HOW almost Everyone can become Moderately RICH, without Telling Any Lies nor Selling Any Capitalist Trash!) By The Worldwide People's Revolution!® Book 001B.

[ ] 40-002 — "What is WRong with those Professing Christians?" (A Self-Examination of the Heart of the Body of Good Government!) By The Worldwide People's Revolution!® Book 002B.

[ ] 40-003 — "For the Love of Money!" (The Strange Things that People Say and Do to Get more Money!) By The Worldwide People's Revolution!® Book 003B.

[ ] 40-004 — "How Best to Prepare for CLIMATE CHANGES!" (The Wisest Plan for Mankind to Follow!) By The Worldwide People's Revolution!® Book 004B.

[ ] 40-005 — "Why do I have to be Surrounded by CRAZY PEOPLE!" (Do almost all People Feel like they are Surrounded by CRAZY People?) By The Worldwide People's Revolution!® Book 005B.

[ ] 40-006 — "The Washington Journal is a FARCE! (C-SPAN Managers are not very WISE!) By The Worldwide People's Revolution!® Book 006C. (This Book has lots of Good Humor.)

[ ] 40-007 — "The PRAYERS of PUMPKINHEADS!" (This Book is otherwise known as the Prayers of Preachers, Priests, Professors, Politicians, Prostitutes, Policemen, Pumpkinheads, Punks, Prisoners, and other Professionals — in other Words, the Capital P People!) By The Worldwide People's Revolution!® Book 007B. (Some of it is for Adults only.)

[ ] 40-008 — "A Sound Argument for Good Masters and Obedient Servants!" (WHY Everyone Needs a Good Master, and every

Master Needs Good Obedient Servants!) By The Worldwide People's Revolution!® Book 008B.

[_] 40-009 — "WHY are some Preachers so POOR?" (HOW almost all Preachers can Get Moderately RICH, without Preaching any Outlandish LIES!) By The Worldwide People's Revolution!® Book 009B.

[_] 40-010 — "GOOD NEWS for REBEL WOMEN!" (HOW almost all Wives can become Moderately RICH without Leaving their Homes! Guaranteed!) By The Worldwide People's Revolution!® Book 010B.

[_] 40-011 — "The Low Court of Supreme Injustices is Brought to Trial!" (Our Selected King Butts Heads with the United States Supreme Court, with or without their Black Robes of Hypocrisies and Lies!) By The Worldwide People's Revolution!® Book 011B. (This Inspired Book contains the Famous *Declaration of Interdependence,* which is a Must Read. It also contains the Correct Wording for the Placard on the Statue of Liberty.)

[_] 40-012 — "The Right Design for Living!" (A List of Great Advantages for Building Beautiful Planned City States!) By The Worldwide People's Revolution!® Book 012B. (This Book contains many Important Drawings, as well as HOW to Save hundreds of Trillions of Dollars by Building Swanky Fortresses, and Living in Peace within them. It is a Companion Book of Book 011B, which contains many more Great Advantages for Swanky Fortresses.)

[_] 40-013 — **"The Gospel According to The Worldwide People's Revolution!®" (The Good News from the Most Modern Perspective!)** See Book 077. (This Book contains the Famous Sermon of Jonah to the Ninevites, whereby 120,000 People Repented in Sackcloth and Ashes! Do not Miss Out on it. Not even the Rev. Dr. Billy Graham got 120,000 Converts during one Day!)

[_] 40-014 — **"Poverty Hunger Riots Strikes Police Brutalities Election Deceptions and Civil Wars!" (The High Price that we Earthlings have Paid for Leaving the Good Land!) By The Worldwide People's Revolution!® Book 014B.**

[_] 40-015 — **"Seven Great Armies of Working Soldiers!" (HOW to Provide a Way for Everyone to WORK: so as to Eliminate Poverty,**

Crimes, Drug Abuses, Prisons and Unnecessary Taxes!) By The Worldwide People's Revolution!® Book 015B. (This Book contains a True-Life Story when the Author was in the Army.)

[_] 40-016 — "The CONSTITUTION for the New RIGHTEOUS One-World Government!" (HOW all Peoples can get True Justice, and Celebrate the Great Year of JUBILEE!) By The Worldwide People's Revolution!® Book 016B.

[_] 40-017 — "The Great World TEMPLE of PEACE!" (The Glory of Jerusalem Arises Again in the Great State of Flexible Texas!) By The Worldwide People's Revolution!® Book 017B.

[_] 40-018 — "The Swanky Associations of Working Soldiers!" (A Fascinating Collection of Various Kinds of Voluntary Working Soldiers!) By The Worldwide People's Revolution!® Book 018B. (There will be thousands of Associations for all Kinds of Occupations, which will Specialize in Fine Arts — such as Hand-carved Leather-bound Books. See "LIGHTNING STRIKES Versus Lightning Bugs!" (HOW you can Become Moderately RICH, without Telling any Lies nor Selling any Trash!) By The Worldwide People's Revolution!® Book 074, for a Picture of a Good Example.)

[_] 40-019 — "GLORIOUS Swanky Hotels Castles and Fortresses!" (Beautiful Planned City States for WISE Intelligent Well-Educated People with Common Sense and Good Understanding!) By The Worldwide People's Revolution!® Book 019B. (This Book contains many Rough Drawings, which could be Greatly Improved upon by someone who Knows the Art, and has the Correct Computer Programs for doing it.)

[_] 40-020 — "Are you a Jobless Graduate of the SKQL uv FQLZ?" (HOW to Get a GOUD EJUKAASHUN without Robbing the Bank!) By The Worldwide People's Revolution!® Book 020B. (This Inspired Book contains the New MAGNIFIED Version {NMV} of *First Corinthians 13,* plus: HOW to Produce Pure Living Water!)

[_] 40-021 — "The LUSCIOUS All-Mineral Organic Method of Gardening!" (HOW to Grow DELICIOUS Satisfying Foods for Potential Kingz and Kweenz in Beautiful Swanky PALACES!) By The Worldwide People's Revolution!® Book 021B. (This Book Explains HOW to make a Flood-proof Garden, while Trapping the Rainwater.)

[_] 40-022 — "Did God or Satan Ordain Medical Doctors?" (Ask Huck Finn and/or Nigger Jim: because neither Tom Sawyer nor Judge Thatcher would Know!) By The Worldwide People's Revolution!® Book 022B. (This Inspired Book Reveals HOW to Prevent Common Colds, and has a Special Chapter that Explains what a True "Nigger" IS. Surprise yourself!)

[_] 40-023 — "The BIG White OUTHOUSE on the Not-so-Biblical Capitol DUNGHILL!" (The Chief Sins of the Divided States of United Lies!) By The Worldwide People's Revolution!® Book 023B. (This Book contains Special Words that most People have never Heard! Surprise yourself again!)

[_] 40-024 — "The Public School of IGNERUNT FQLZ!" (HOW we have been GRAATLEE DISEEVD by Capitalism!) By The Worldwide People's Revolution!® Book 024B. (This Book Teaches Children HOW to "Reed and Riit in Funetik Ingglish in just wun Daa!" You should Challenge your Frendz and Naaberz with it.)

[_] 40-025 — "In thu Beeginingz uv Thingz!" (Thu Kreeaashun Stooree frum thu Beegining!) By The Worldwide People's Revolution!® Book 025B. {The Original Cover Photo showed a Picture of a Golden Supootaa (Sapote), which not one Person in a Million has ever Tasted: because it does not Ship very well, in spite of it being one of the most Sweetest Pleasant Fruits known to Mankind, which must Ripen on the Tree to be Extremely Good, after it is Grown Properly by "The LUSCIOUS All-Mineral Organic Method of Gardening!" Book 021B, which Means that the Topsoil must have all of the Proper Minerals in it. Remember the Grapes of Eschol, which the Children of Israel brought back from the Promised Land in the *Book of Joshua,* which Required 2 Strong Men to Carry just one Cluster! See the Fascinating Photos in: "Orgimmick Gardening at its Best!" (HOW to Grow Delicious Satisfying Foods without a 10 Million-Dollar Investment!) By The Worldwide People's Revolution!® Book 079.}

[_] 40-026 — "God Speaks and the Whole World Listens!" (Fire on the Mountain from the Burning Bush by the Spirit of Truths!) By The Worldwide People's Revolution!® Book 026B. (This Powerful Book contains the Best Noah Story of all of the Books, including that of Gilgamesh the Great of Ancient Babylon!)

[_] 40-027 — "Does a Good Soldier have to be a MURDERER?" (Seven Great Swanky Armies of Voluntary Working Soldiers!) By

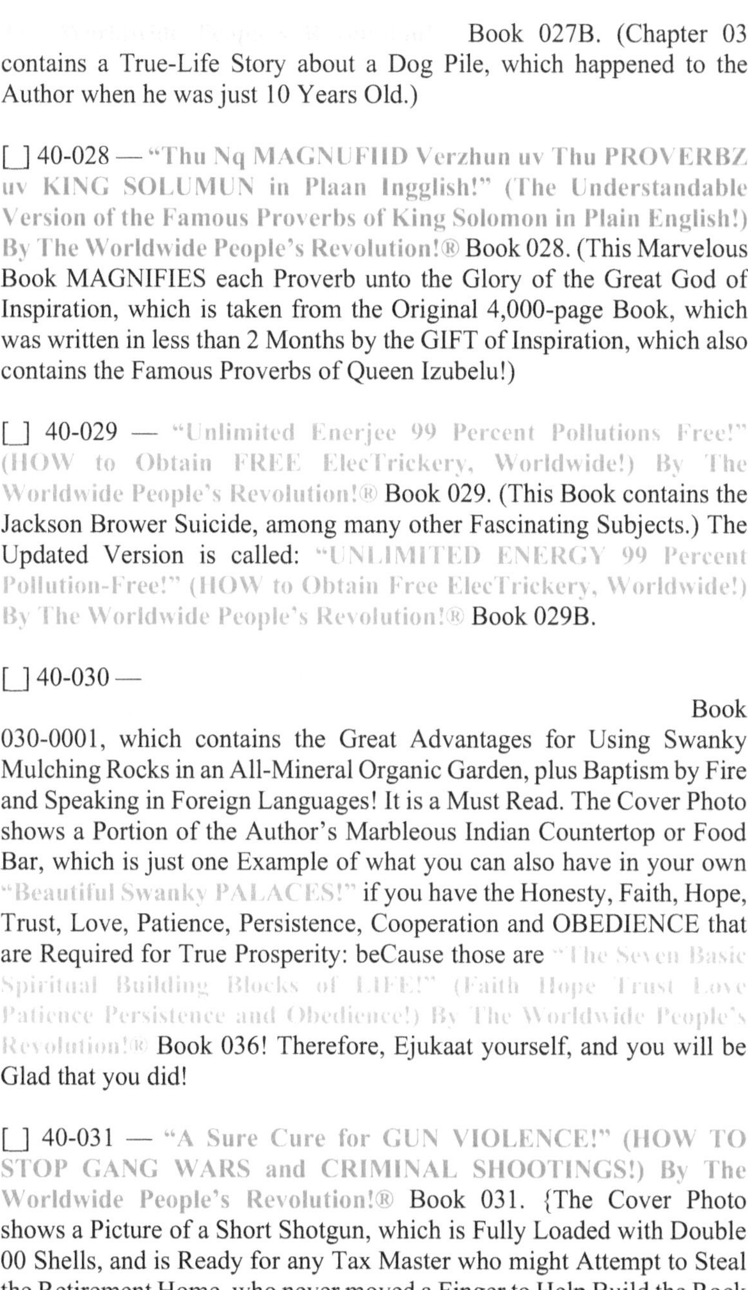

Book 027B. (Chapter 03 contains a True-Life Story about a Dog Pile, which happened to the Author when he was just 10 Years Old.)

[_] 40-028 — "Thu Nq MAGNUFIID Verzhun uv Thu PROVERBZ uv KING SOLUMUN in Plaan Ingglish!" (The Understandable Version of the Famous Proverbs of King Solomon in Plain English!) By The Worldwide People's Revolution!® Book 028. (This Marvelous Book MAGNIFIES each Proverb unto the Glory of the Great God of Inspiration, which is taken from the Original 4,000-page Book, which was written in less than 2 Months by the GIFT of Inspiration, which also contains the Famous Proverbs of Queen Izubelu!)

[_] 40-029 — "Unlimited Enerjee 99 Percent Pollutions Free!" (HOW to Obtain FREE ElecTrickery, Worldwide!) By The Worldwide People's Revolution!® Book 029. (This Book contains the Jackson Brower Suicide, among many other Fascinating Subjects.) The Updated Version is called: "UNLIMITED ENERGY 99 Percent Pollution-Free!" (HOW to Obtain Free ElecTrickery, Worldwide!) By The Worldwide People's Revolution!® Book 029B.

[_] 40-030 —

Book 030-0001, which contains the Great Advantages for Using Swanky Mulching Rocks in an All-Mineral Organic Garden, plus Baptism by Fire and Speaking in Foreign Languages! It is a Must Read. The Cover Photo shows a Portion of the Author's Marbleous Indian Countertop or Food Bar, which is just one Example of what you can also have in your own "Beautiful Swanky PALACES!" if you have the Honesty, Faith, Hope, Trust, Love, Patience, Persistence, Cooperation and OBEDIENCE that are Required for True Prosperity: beCause those are "The Seven Basic Spiritual Building Blocks of LIFE!" (Faith Hope Trust Love Patience Persistence and Obedience!) By The Worldwide People's Revolution!® Book 036! Therefore, Ejukaat yourself, and you will be Glad that you did!

[_] 40-031 — "A Sure Cure for GUN VIOLENCE!" (HOW TO STOP GANG WARS and CRIMINAL SHOOTINGS!) By The Worldwide People's Revolution!® Book 031. {The Cover Photo shows a Picture of a Short Shotgun, which is Fully Loaded with Double 00 Shells, and is Ready for any Tax Master who might Attempt to Steal the Retirement Home, who never moved a Finger to Help Build the Rock Houses, whereby we moved more than 66,666,666 Pounds by Hand, whose Property was Cunningly Stolen by that False Anti-Christ WICKED Cover-up Government, which allowed Bankers to Rob us of 30 Years of Hard Labor and more than 300,000 dollars-worth of Investments in our Uncommon American Farm, which is Explained in: "LIGHTNING STRIKES Versus Lightning Bugs!" (HOW you can Become Moderately RICH, without Telling any Lies nor Selling any Trash!) By The Worldwide People's Revolution!® Book 074, which contains many Photographs with Profound Explanations! Do not be left out in the Darkness of Ignorance. Get Informed, now: beCause, **"The Great False Economy is now DEBUNKED!"** Book 053.}

[ ] 40-032 — "AIIRMWVC and Reasonable Solutions!" (Aliens, Illegal Immigrants, Refugees, Migrant Workers and other Victims of Capitalism!) By The Worldwide People's Revolution!® Book 032. (This Inspired Book contains *the New MAGNIFIED Version of Job 33*.)

[ ] 40-033 — "MARK TWAIN Races for the PRESIDENCY with a Landslide VICTORY!" (The 2020 Presidential Candidates Desperately Need Some STRONG Undefeatable COMPETITION!) By The Worldwide People's Revolution!® Book 033B. {This Book contains a Part of the Author's Autobiography, and his Personal Answers to the Questions in: "The Complete SURVEYS of our VALUES!" (SURVEYS of Religious Spiritual Political Governmental Sexual Social Moral Economic Business Labor Habitual and Miscellaneous VALUES!) Book 059. **The CONDENSED Version** is Book 033C, which most People Prefer.}

[ ] 40-034 — "ECCLESIASTES Uncovered and Recovered!" (The New MAGNIFIED Version of Ecclesiastes and the Song of Solomon in Plain English!) By The Worldwide People's Revolution!® Book 034. (This is the Book that contains the Famous Sayings for *"There is a Time to be Born, and a Time to Die ..."* which has been Greatly Magnified!)

[ ] 40-035 — "The Environmentalists' Perfect Paradise!" (HOW almost Everyone can be Living in a Beautiful Manmade Paradise!) By The Worldwide People's Revolution!® Book 035C. (This Book contains the NMV of *Psalm 48,* which will Amaze you, O Lady Doubtfulness!)

[ ] 40-036 — "The Seven Basic Spiritual Building Blocks of LIFE!" (Faith Hope Trust Love Patience Persistence and Obedience!) By The Worldwide People's Revolution!® Book 036. (This Book contains

the Mockingbird's Version of *Hebrews 11,* plus the NMV of *First Corinthians 13,* among many other "Goodies.")

[_] 40-037 — "DIETS!" (A Reasonable Solution for the "Eternal Controversy"!) By The Worldwide People's Revolution!® Book 037.

[_] 40-038 — "The Nature of CAPITALISM!" (A List of the EVILS of CAPITALISM!) By The Worldwide People's Revolution!® Book 038.

[_] 40-039 — "SWANGKEENOMIKS Rules the Roost!" (HOW all People can Prosper in a RIIT WAA, and STOP Polluting the Earth with Capitalist TRASH!) By The Worldwide People's Revolution!® Book 039. (The Cover Photo shows a Portion of the Author's Retirement Home, before the 5,000+ square-feet Concrete Roof was Installed, after moving more than 66 Million Pounds by Hand, and mostly by his own Boastful Hands!)

[_] 40-040 — "The New MAGNIFIED Version of The Book of MORMON!" (The Story of the White and Dark Indians in the Americas!) By Big Chief Standsover Bull in River of Life! Book 040, which comes in 2 Volumes of about 500 Pages, each. The Cover Photo on the First Volume shows the Queen of England's Golden Coach, and the Cover Photo on the Second Volume shows one of many Polished Spanish Marble Walls in our Selected King's Retirement Home, which is worth a thousand dollars per square yard, which is another Example of what you can also have, if you simply OBEY your Righteous KING! All such Marble is very Inspiring. No one could Study it for very long without Believing in a Great Creator God. The Picture does not do it Justice. You would have to See it in Person, and Wash it with Pure Water to bring Out the Beauty of it.

[_] 40-041 — "The GREAT Worldwide TELEVISED Court HEARING!" (That Great Meeting of the Most-Intelligent and Well-Educated Minds!) By The Worldwide People's Revolution!® Book 041B. {This is the Book that the World has long been Waiting for: beCause it will Overthrow the Evil Empires, and make it Possible to Establish "The New RIGHTEOUS One-World Government!" (HOW to Establish a Righteous One-World Government without Going to WAR!) By The Worldwide People's Revolution!® Book 056. This is the Greatest Idea since the Invention of the Light Bulb, Guaranteed!}

[_] 40-042 — "The Secret City of the Great King!" (HOW the True Church will Escape from the Great Tribulation!) By The Worldwide People's Revolution!® Book 042. (Be Sure to Inform your Friends, Relatives and Naaberz about this Wonderful Book: beCause they might also Want to Escape!)

[_] 40-043 — "Terrorists Beware that your Days are Numbered!" (HOW to Bring those Terrorist Attacks to a Screeching HALT!) By The Worldwide People's Revolution!® Book 043. (This Book also contains the Fascinating Book of LEHI, which has now been Restored!) †‡

[_] 40-044 — "The New MAGNIFIED Version of ISAIAH in Plain English!" (The Understandable Version of the Book of Isaiah!) By The Worldwide People's Revolution!® Book 044. (The Cover Photo shows a Swanky Potato and Avocado Salad with Sweet Peas and Corn, among other "Secret" Ingredients, which are Revealed within the Book. Remember that you can read many Words for Free in the Book Previews on www.Amazon.com.usa or UK.)

[_] 40-045 — "HOW to Become a HOLY Man!" (40 Good Reasons WHY People Should FAST and PRAY!) By The Worldwide People's Revolution!® Book 045, which is a Companion Book of:

[_] 40-046 — "The Proper RULES for FASTING!" (The Complete Instruction Manual for True Repentance!) By The Worldwide People's Revolution!® Book 046, which is a Companion Book of the above-mentioned Book, which contains a True-Life Story about an Old Black Mare called Lucy, who Fasted for 30 Days without Food nor Water, who was Physiologically "Born Again," as Jesus might say. See the Full Details in: "The New MAGNIFIED Version of The GOOD NEWS According to Saint JOHN!" (The Gospel According to Saint John Zebedee Boanerges in Plain English!) Book 062, which contains many Inspiring Photographs with Explanations!

[_] 40-047 — "Are Americans the Most-STUPID People who ever Lived?" (HOW Working People can PROSPER and Live in PEACE Under the Rulership of a RIGHTEOUS KING!) By The Worldwide People's Revolution!® Book 047. (The Cover Photo shows a large Portion of the Author's Living Room Floor, which is worth 100,000$, which is just another Good Example of what you can also have, just for Loving and Obeying your Elected King!)

[_] 40-048 — "An Amazing Collection of Wit and Wisdom!" (The Marvelous Tale of the Colorful Peacock from Angel Ridge, and the Strong Rope of Everlasting Hope!) By The Worldwide People's Revolution!® Book 048. (The Cover Photo shows a Book Display, which will be Greatly Enhanced during the Future, when all 364+ Inspired Books are on Display in a Swanky Truth-brary, as Opposed to the Public LIE-brary.)

[_] 40-049 — "Justifications for Capitalizations!" (WHY our Selected King DEFIES the School of FOOLS by Capitalizing LOVE and HATE!) By The Worldwide People's Revolution!® Book 049.

[_] 40-050 — "The END of CONFUSION!" (The Great CELEBRATION of the Magnificent Wedding of the Most-Humble, Honest Nations, and the Grand Year of JUBILEE!) By The Worldwide People's Revolution!® Book 050. (Just Try to Visualize those **"Seven Great Swanky Armies of Voluntary Working Soldiers"** Marching through the Valley of Megiddo, being Dressed in their Colorful Robes, while the Band Plays *The Battle Hymn of the Republic,* and the Choirs Sing the Praises of the Great KING of Kings! What a Sight and Sound that will be, which will be Climaxed in "The Great World TEMPLE of PEACE," when the Nations will get Married, along with our Elected King! Come one, come all to "The GREAT Worldwide TELEVISED Court HEARING," by Means of your Wide Flat-screen TVs, whereby you might Learn WHY, WHEN and HOW!) †‡

[_] 40-051 — "The Loathsome Burdens of the Independent Jackasses!" (A New Civilized Approach for Quietly Solving our Massive Problems!) By The Worldwide People's Revolution!® Book 051. (Just Think about the Multitude of almost Worthless Meetings of the Minds, who Strained themselves to Think of Reasonable Solutions for our Massive Problems, who sometimes even Prayed to God for Help; but, the Best Solutions have been here for no less than 40 Years — Thanks to the Spirit of Inspiration from GOD!)

[_] 40-052 — "Are we Tax Slaves of a Lower Order than those Lying Conniving EDOMITES!" (HOW to be Liberated From all Forms of Slavery, Worldwide!) By The Worldwide People's Revolution!® Book 052B. {This Inspired Book once had another Title and Author, which was not Acceptable by Amazon, which has now been Restored in all of its Glory, and is Published by more Trustworthy People, who are not Afraid of Controversies, nor of: "The Swanky Sword of Divine

Truths!" (The Most-Powerful Weapon in the Whole Universe!) By The Worldwide People's Revolution!® Book 067.}

[_] 40-053 — "The Great False Economy is now DEBUNKED!" (Adolf Hitler had a much Better Economic System!) By The Worldwide People's Revolution!® Book 053. {Trust me, Adolf was no Saint; but, during the Day of God's Judgment, he will be Justified, while his Anti-Christ Opponents will be Condemned: beCause they Refused to Attend a Worldwide Radio Debate with Adolf Hitler, whose Arguments will Stand Up during the Day of Judgment, which would have Prevented World War 2, and thus Saved the Lives of no less than 60 Million People! Likewise, we Tax Slaves must now Act more Wisely, and DEMAND "The GREAT Worldwide TELEVISED Court HEARING," Book 041B, whereby we might Save the World from that Dreadful Battle of Megiddo, called *Armageddon!* Yes, the Ball is now in YOUR Hands, O Potential Friend or Enemy, and you are now Responsible for it. Therefore, do not Shirk your Duty as a Free Citizen; but, Help us to Spread this Message, far and wide, whereby the Masses of People will be Demanding The GWTCH, and thus, Prevent "The Great ATOMIC NIGHTMARE!" (The Saddest Story in World History!) By The Great White Bald Eagle! Book 099.}

[_] 40-054 — "The UGLY Scarred Dishonest Face of Poor Old Miserable UNCLE SAM!" (A Memorial Day Legacy!) By The Worldwide People's Revolution!® Book 054. {NOTE: This Inspired Book was also Suppressed by Amazon, who will be most Ashamed of themselves if they do not Un-suppress it during the Future: beCause it will also be Published by People of Greater Faith, who Know for a Fact that it is the TRUTH! Therefore, just be Patient. Search for Book 054B, *King James Version.*}

[_] 40-055 — "The United States of the Whole World!" (A True Global Economy for the Masses of Working People!) By The Worldwide People's Revolution!® Book 055. (This Inspired Book contains many Colored Photographs with Explanations. It is a Good Book to Publish in Foreign Nations, who are not so Blinded by their Pride, who can See the Mountain of Lies much Better at a Distance from them: beCause of not being a Part of the American Corruption.) †‡

[_] 40-056 — "The New RIGHTEOUS One-World Government!" (HOW to Establish a Righteous One-World Government without Going to WAR!) By The Worldwide People's Revolution!® Book

056. (This is a KEY Book, which everyone should Study Carefully and Prayerfully.)

[_] 40-057 —

Book 057. {NOTE: Many Professing "Christians" Falsely Claim that their so-called *"Holy Bibles"* do not Contain any Contradictions, being "the Infallible Inspired Word of the Living God," but, without the Capitalized Words, and without Explaining just WHY there are more than 200 Contradictory Versions of it! This Book Reveals how to Deal with those Biblical Problems, and come to Understand WHY God Allowed it to Happen for the Truth's Sake. Trust God: beCause, you have never Heard this Explanation before now. See also: "C-SPAN-DEX!" (Your Filtered View of Bad Government!) By The Worldwide People's Revolution!® Book 097.}

[_] 40-058 — "The Divided States of United Lies!" (The so-called "United States of North America" in Disguise!) By The Worldwide People's Revolution!® Book 058. {NOTE: This is perhaps the most Referred to Book among all of the Books by our Selected King; but, that does not Mean that it is his Best Book by any Means, which is Well Camouflaged: so that it will Survive the Test of Time, even if the others are BURNED by the Anti-Christ Followers of Satan, who are Possession Worshipers of the Worst Kind, who Seek to Justify American Lies, rather than Quickly Confess them, and thus Escape from their Self-made Prison of Propagandish Lies! Just be Perfectly Honest, and you will have no Problem with any of our Literature.}

[_] 40-059 — "The Complete SURVEYS of our VALUES!" (SURVEYS of Religious Spiritual Political Governmental Sexual Social Moral Economical Business Labor Habitual and Miscellaneous VALUES!) By The Worldwide People's Revolution!® Book 059. {NOTE: According to our Selected King, every Potential Leader in the World must Fill Out and File those Surveys on the Internet for everyone to Study, whereby the Best People might be Elected by those Wise People who have also Filled Out the Simplistic Surveys of their own Values, whereby they will be Qualified to VOTE. Otherwise, they will not be Qualified to Vote, which will Eliminate a LOT of Wasted Money on Election Deceptions, while at the same Time it will Educate a lot of Ignorant People, who Desperately Need to Study that Inspired Book before Voting for another Dimwitcrat, Reprobate, or Independent Jackass!}

[_] 40-059B — "The Simplistic SURVEYS of our VALUES!" Book 059B. (The Cover Photo shows some Beautiful African Antelopes, who are Free with a Capital F.)

[_] 40-060 — "HOW to Get our PRIORITIES in ORDER!" (The Glories of Democracy; and, Does DEMON-ocracy have its Priorities in Order?) By The Worldwide People's Revolution!® Book 060. This Book will need to be Re-written by a Collective Group of Wise People, who will Contribute their True-Life Stories during the Future, when they Wake Up and come to their Right Senses with the Prodigal Son of *Luke 15*. See:

[_] 40-061 — "The New MAGNIFIED Version of The GOOD NEWS According to Saint LUKE!" (The Magnified Gospel of Saint Luke in Plain English!) By The Worldwide People's Revolution!® Book 061, which is by Far the Best Version of that Gospel on the Earth, which has no Rivals at all among the other 200+ Versions. Guaranteed!

[_] 40-062 — "The New MAGNIFIED Version of The GOOD NEWS According to Saint JOHN!" (The Gospel According to Saint John Zebedee Boanerges [pronounced Boo-an-er-jeez] in Plain English!) By The Worldwide People's Revolution!® Book 062, which also has no Rivals among all of the other Versions: beCause this is no Translation of anything; but, it is the Inspired Words of the Living God, which were Revealed by the Holy Spirit to our Selected King, who has not Died, yet.

[_] 40-063 — "The New MAGNIFIED Version of the Book of ACTS!" (The Understandable Version of the Acts of the Apostles in Plain English!) By The Worldwide People's Revolution!® Book 063. (This Inspired Book makes it Understandable WHY the Jews Hated the Apostles so much. You will have to Read it to Believe it.)

[_] 40-064 — "The New MAGNIFIED Version of the PSALMS of King David!" (The Understandable Version of the Famous Psalms in Plain English!) By The Worldwide People's Revolution!® Book 064. You will be Amazed!

[_] 40-065 — "A List of FAIR Swanky Wages!" (The Equitable Wage System!) By The Worldwide People's Revolution!® Book 065. (All Hardworking People will LOVE this Good Book! You will also, if you Study it Carefully.)

[_] 40-066 — "Beautiful Swanky PALACES!" (A New Concept in Living Habits — Swanky Palaces for Poor People!) By The Worldwide People's Revolution!® Book 066. (You have no Idea what a "Swanky Palace" IS, unless you have read this Unique Book, or another one that Describes those Palaces, and several of them do; but, this one has the Best Description. ENJOY!)

[_] 40-067 — "The Swanky Sword of Divine Truths!" (The Most-Powerful Weapon in the Whole Universe!) By The Worldwide People's Revolution!® Book 067. (The very Reason that our Selected King has no Rivals is beCause of the Swanky Sword of Divine Truths, which no one can Defeat by any Means. Therefore, you Need to have it on your own Side, whereby no one can Defeat your Arguments! Be Strong, be Brave, have Faith and put on the Whole Armor of GOD!)

[_] 40-068 — "Has your Life become Extremely Complicated?" (HOW to Live a SIMPLE Life!) By The Worldwide People's Revolution!® Book 068. (Many People are not even Aware of just how Complicated their Lives are, until suddenly they are ready to Commit Suicide! It is Best to Prevent all such Evil Things, and this Book tells HOW.)

[_] 40-069 — "The IDEAL Place to Live!" (HOW to Discover the Ideal Place to Live!) By The Worldwide People's Revolution!® Book 069. {NOTE: Our Selected King Searched the World over, and did not Discover any Idea Place to Live. Therefore, he Concluded that we must Make our own. Yes, we must Build those "GLORIOUS Swanky Hotels Castles and Fortresses!" (Beautiful Planned City States for WISE Intelligent Well-Educated People with Common Sense and Good Understanding!) By The Worldwide People's Revolution!® Book 019B, even if we must DRAFT "Seven Great Armies of Working Soldiers!" (HOW to Provide a Way for Everyone to WORK: so as to Eliminate Poverty, Crimes, Drug Abuses, Prisons and Unnecessary Taxes!) By The Worldwide People's Revolution!® Book 015B; and what on this Good Earth could Prove to be more Profitable than that, and without going to WAR?}

[_] 40-070 — "Our Elected King Who Speaks Out!" (It is High Time for some Sane Person to Get Control of this Insane World!) By The Worldwide People's Revolution!® Book 070. (This Inspired Book contains a Special Speech that is Addressed to both Houses of the Congress in Washington. You will Love it, O Honest Man of Greater Faith!)

[_] 40-071 — "How GAY is GOD?" (Oh, the Wonders of it all, when it ALL Hangs Out!) By The Worldwide People's Revolution!® Book 071. (Do not Judge the Book, until you have Carefully "Red" all of it. You will be Surprised by the Provable Truths within it, and Greatly Humored by the Author's Exceptionally Good Humor, who is less Gay than God, who has never had any Sexual Intercourse during his entire Life! In other Words, he is a VIRGIN!)

[_] 40-072 — "LIGHTNING STRIKES Versus Lightning Bugs and Impotent Fireflies!" (A Memorial Photo Album of some Real American Heroes!) By The Worldwide People's Revolution!® Book 072. (NOTE: This Book is Unique among all of the Books by our Selected King: beCause he did not get to Proof-read it before the Computer Crashed. It just Happened to be Saved on a Computer Chip before the Computer Crashed, and therefore it was Saved in PDF. But, the Corrections did not get made, which makes it a Special Collector's Item, which has more than 100 Colored Photos, which was what Caused the Crash.) †‡

[_] 40-073 — "The BEST of CAPITALISM!" (Corrections for: "LIGHTNING STRIKES Versus Lightning Bugs and Impotent Fireflies!") Book 073. (It is a completely new Book, except for those Corrections; and it is one of the Best Books in the World, which all Honest People will Love.)

[_] 40-074 — "LIGHTNING STRIKES Versus Lightning Bugs!" (HOW you can Become Moderately RICH, without Telling any Lies nor Selling any Trash!) By The Worldwide People's Revolution!® Book 074, which is the Perfection of all of the Lightning Striking Books, which is Recommended above all others for Mass Production: beCause it stands the Best Chance of being a Real Winner, just after this Book that you are now Reading, which has a Magnetizing Title!

[_] 40-075 — "What are the PUNISHMENTS for Dietary Sins?" (Have we Served ourselves Well at the Tables of our Lusts?) By The Worldwide People's Revolution!® Book 075. (This Book is too Controversial to be Published at this Time. Be very Patient until it is Available: beCause it is HOT!)

[_] 40-076 — "What is WRong with those CRAZY CHRISTIANS?" (A Self-Examination of the Heart of the Body of Good Government!) By The Worldwide People's Revolution!® Book 076.

[_] 40-077 — "The Gospel According to our Elected King!" (The Good News from the Most Modern Perspective!) By The Worldwide People's Revolution!® Book 077. (This is perhaps the Best Book that you will Discover on Amazon, which contains the Famous Sermon that Jonah gave to the Ninevites, plus a very Special Sermon by Jesus Christ, himself, which is taken from the Dead Sea Scrolls! It is simply a Marvelous Book that everyone must "Reed." ENJOY!) ‡

[_] 40-078 — "The Root Cause for almost all Evils!" (The Strange Things that People Say and Do to Get more Money!) By The Worldwide People's Revolution!® Book 078. (This Book contains many Colored Photographs with Fascinating Explanations!)

[_] 40-079 — "Orgimmick Gardening at its Best!" (HOW to Grow Delicious Satisfying Foods without a 10-Million-Dollar Investment!) By The Worldwide People's Revolution!® Book 079. (This Book also contains many Colored Photographs with Wonderful Explanations!)

[_] 40-080 — "Guaranteed Solutions!" (HOW to Solve our Local and Global Problems in the Most-Rational Manner Possible!) By The Worldwide People's Revolution!® Book 080. (See the Description on Amazon: because they Offer a ONE-MILLION-DOLLAR REWARD to anyone who can Prove our Selected King's Solutions to be WRong or Unworkable! Can you Beat that? Do you have all such Guaranteed Solutions? Does any Politician? Only our Selected King has those Provable Solutions: beCause God Blest him with them, which can be Proven in any Courtroom with Law and Order. ENJOY!)

[_] 40-081 — "Mexicans are more Intelligent than Americans!" (A Unique Challenge to all Americans and Mexicans!) By The Worldwide People's Revolution!® Book 081. {NOTE: The Remaining 275 Inspired Books by the Author of this Book may only be found in English, until we can get them Properly Translated into other Languages. Shame on you People who Killed him, who Broke his Heart with your Unbelief. May God have Mercy on your Poor Wretched Souls.} †§‡

[_] 40-081B — "¡Los Mexicanos son más Inteligentes que los Estadounidenses!" (¡Un Desafío Único para todos los Estadounidenses y Mexicanos!) By The Worldwide People's Revolution!® Book 082. {NOTA: Aquí está el primer Libro en Español, que puede no ser Perfecto; pero, es Perfectamente lo Suficientemente Bueno para Iluminar las Mentes de quien lo Estudia.}

[_] 40-082 — "The Process of Making a RIGHTEOUS KING!" (A Fascinating Autobiography of our Selected King!) By The Worldwide People's Revolution!® Book 082. {NOTE: He once had a 6,000-plus-page Autobiography, called: **"DIARRHEA of the Mind!"** which gave Details of his entire Life, since he was only 4 Years Old, when he had an Encounter with God, which has been Lost: beCause those Backup Disks became Obsolete, and were thus Trashed, along with the Obsolete Computer, which Costed 4,000-plus Dollars, along with the Hewlett-Packard Printer, which Costed another 4,000-plus Dollars, whose Antiquated Software would not Work with a Modern Computer, nor did Hewlett have an Updated Software Program for it: beCause they are Capitalist Scammers, who should be put Out of Business for Practicing Donald Trump Tactics! See: "The Nature of CAPITALISM!" (A List of the EVILS of CAPITALISM!) By The Worldwide People's Revolution!® Book 038.}

[_] 40-083 — "Was Billy Graham Greatly Deceived?" (Giving Honor to whom Honor is Due!) By The Worldwide People's Revolution!® Book 083. {NOTE: If you know a Grahamite, please Direct him or her to this Inspired Book, whereby he or she might be Converted to the Truths within it, and thus be Saved from Grahamite Perversions. Thank you in Advance. They will also Thank you for it: beCause they Suffer so Needlessly, when they should be Free, Healthy and Happy, like our Selected King, who has no Aches nor Pains, who used to Work Hard all Day long, and not be Weary, just like you can Reed in *the Book of Isaiah 40:31, NMV!*}

[_] 40-084 — "The New MAGNIFIED Version of the Book of DEUTERONOMY!" (The Understandable Version of Deuteronomy in Plain English!) Book 084. This is actually one of the Best Books within the entire Holy Bible, and also one of the Longest; but, do not allow that Fact to Deter you by any Means: beCause, "the Bigger Book is Normally a Better Book," which is True of a lot of Books, including all of the above Books: beCause it is the Nature of the Holy Spirit to get into Long-winded Sermons, you might say, which is WHY the Apostle Paul Preached until Midnight in *the Book of Acts,* until some Boy went to Sleep and Fell from a Window and Killed himself, whom the Apostle Paul Raised Up from the Dead and went on Preaching until the Dawn of the Day! And it is NOT Jewish Mythology! †§‡§§ {See: "The New MAGNIFIED Version of the Book of ACTS" for the Finest of Details, Book 063.}

[_] 40-085 — "All of the Arguments are in Favor of our Selected King, who has Zero Challengers!" (Before you Attend another Election Deception, you should Carefully Study this Inspired Book with an Honest Open Mind!) By The Worldwide People's Revolution!® Book 085.

[_] 40-086 — "Provable Truths that True Christians cannot Rightly Deny!" (A Fair Challenge for all Professing "Christians" to Meditate on with Honest Open Minds!) By The Worldwide People's Revolution!® Book 086.

[_] 40-087 — "How all Women can Get True Justice without Getting Divorced from God!" (The Unjust Case of Judge Brett Kavanaugh and Doctor Christine Blasey Ford is now Revisited by a Wise Son of King Solomon!) By The Worldwide People's Revolution!® B-087.

[_] 40-088 — "The New MAGNIFIED Version of GENESIS!" (The Enlightening Version of the Beginnings of Things!) By The Worldwide People's Revolution!® Book 088.

[_] 40-089 — "The New MAGNIFIED Version of the HOLY KORAN!" (WHY MuhamMAD went to Hell for Spiritual MURDER!) By The Worldwide People's Revolution!® Book 089. This is by Far the Best Version of the *Holy Koran,* which is Loved by all Honest Muslims, Hindus, Christians and Buddhists, Worldwide! Surprise yourself and others. Ask them what it Means? §‡

[_] 40-090 — "A New Jerusalem in the Great State of Flexible Texas!" (HOW to make Good Use of the Mississippi River!) By The Worldwide People's Revolution!® Book 090. This Book contains many Fascinating Photos of God's Handiwork. ENJOY!

[_] 40-091 — "What is The GREATEST SIN?" (And it is NOT Blasphemy Against the Holy Spirit!) By The Worldwide People's Revolution!® Book 091.

[_] 40-092 — "HOW to Make America (and all other Nations) Really GREAT Without Telling any LIES!" (The Founding Fathers would have Loved it!) By The Worldwide People's Revolution!® Book 092.

[_] 40-093 — "HOW Righteousness can Overcome Wickedness!" (The Triumph of the Soul who Knows God!) By The Enlightened Professor of Common Sense! Book 093. {Notice how the Calves in the

93

Cover Photo Segregated themselves by their Colors, from Left to Right. God Guided them. ‡}

[_] 40-094 — "Justifications for MAGNIFICATIONS!" (The Problem with Understanding a Complicated Contradictory Mutilated Unholy Bible!) Or: (The Problem with Inventing Lies that are too BIG to DIE!) By The Worldwide People's Revolution!® Book 094.

[_] 40-095 — "HOW to IDENTIFY God's Elected Ones!" (Are YOU one of the Elect?) By The Worldwide People's Revolution!® Book 095.

[_] 40-096 — "GOVERNMENT Versus Independence!" (How Much CONTROL Should a Government Have?") By The Worldwide People's Revolution!® Book 096.

[_] 40-097 — "C-SPAN-DEX!" (Your Filtered View of Bad Government!) By The Worldwide People's Revolution!® Book 097.

[_] 40-098 — "Profitable Swanky MULCHING ROCKS!" (30 Advantages for Using Swanky Mulching Rocks in an All-Mineral Organic Garden!) By The Worldwide People's Revolution!® Book 098. {Just Think, the School of Fools never Mentioned them, nor did the False Government, nor any of the False Churches: beCause they are Uneducated and Foolish.}

[_] 40-099 — "The Great ATOMIC NIGHTMARE!" (The Saddest Story in World History!) By The Great White Bald Eagle! Book 099. {NOTE: Let us Hope and Pray that no one ever has to Write this Book; but, if they Do, it should Spook the Devil Out of you!}

[_] 40-100 — "Our Selected King SPEAKS OUT!" (It is High Time for some Sane Person to get Total Control of this Insane World!) By The Worldwide People's Revolution!® Book 100!

[_] 40-101 — "What will you Do when the Rain STOPS?" (God's Last Resort to Save Mankind from his MADNESS!) By The Worldwide People's Revolution!® Book 101!

[_] 40-102 — "Beautiful Swanky Stone Dome Home COMPLEXES!" (HOW to Build SECURE Tax-proof, Insurance-proof, Self-air-conditioned, Paint-proof, Rot-proof, Termite-proof, Mouse-proof, Fireproof, Tornado-proof, Hurricane-proof, Thief-proof, and BOMB-PROOF Houses!) By The Worldwide People's Revolution!® Book 102.

[_] 40-103 — "Royal Swanky Buffets!" (The Best Feasts in the Whole World!) By The Worldwide People's Revolution!® Book 103.

[_] 40-104 — "101 Good Reasons and Great Advantages for Establishing a Righteous One-World Government!" (Government By the People, Of the People, and For the People!) By The Worldwide People's Revolution!® Book 104. This Book Suggests thousands of Good Reasons and Great Advantages. But, of course, you have to be Able to THINK, which seems to be something that Wicked Politicians cannot Do, or Refuse to Do; and neither can most Preachers and Teachers Do it. Therefore, this Inspired Book will Help them to Think and Remember.

[_] 40-105 — "The New MAGNIFIED Version of the Book of REVELATION!" (The Understandable Version of the Most-Controversial Book in the Whole World!) By The Worldwide People's Revolution!® Book 105. This Proverbial "Bombshell" will be Published just before the Second Coming of Jesus Christ! Get your Seatbelts Fastened! Be Prepared for Radical Changes!

[_] 40-106 — **"The Naked Glory of Beautiful Mankind!" (1,000 Pages of Sheer Artistic BEAUTY!) By The Worldwide People's Revolution!®** Book 106. (See Book 014B-02-09-T for the Explanation.)

[_] 40-107 — **"The Beautiful Faces of Holy Men!" (The very Best that God has to Offer!) By The Worldwide People's Revolution!®** Book 107.

[_] 40-108 — "The Worldwide People's Revolution!" (A Comprehensive Plan for Obtaining Worldwide Law, Order, Obedience, Peace and True Prosperity!) By The Worldwide People's Revolution!® Book 108.

[_] 40-109 — "VOTE for The GOAT!" (The New Political Party that has Guaranteed Solutions for our Massive Problems!) By The Worldwide People's Revolution!® Book 109.

[_] 40-110 — "IMPORTANT THINGS that Should Have Been Written in the Holy Bible!" (A Special Challenge to all Professing Christians, Jews, Hindus, Muslims and Atheists!) **By The Irreverent Penname Scumbag!** Book 110.

[_] 40-111 — "Hosts of HOAXES Live In Under Around and Over the Little White OUTHOUSE!" (WHY Spiritually-Blind Cowardly-Americans are Hunkering Down in their Empty Root Cellars!) **By The Irreverent Penname Oversight!** Book 111.

[_] 40-112 — "Should Wives Obey their Husbands?" (OR, Should Husbands OBEY their Wives?) **By The Irreverent Penname Mockingbird!** Book 112.

[_] 40-113 — "Modern Deceived SLAVES!" (10 Simple Steps for Liberating ALL Modern Slaves, Worldwide, Including Yourself!) **By Liberty and Justice for ALL!** Book 113.

[_] 40-114 — "Are you a Jobless Graduate of the School of Fools?" (How to Obtain a Good Education without Robbing the Bank, Selling any Trash, nor Telling any Lies!) **By The Professor Wordcraft Enlightenment!** Book 114.

[_] 40-115 — "Beautiful Swanky FASTING SANITARIUMS!" (HOW to Learn Good Self-Discipline!) **By The Worldwide People's Revolution!®** Book 115.

[_] 40-116 — "Swanky Institutions for Compassionate Corrections!" (How to Correct even the Most-Stubborn Bullies!) **By The Biggest Bully of All Bullies!** Book 116.

[_] 40-117 — "What is True PROGRESS???" (Are we Making any True Progress, at all?) **By The Worldwide People's Revolution!®** Book 117.

[_] 40-118 — "Is America a White Nation with a Black Heart?" (How to Separate Truth from Fiction!) **By The Good Pastor of Uncommon Sense!** Book 118.

[_] 40-119 — "Which Church is the Right Church?" (Can all Churches be Correct?) **By The Good Pastor of Uncommon Sense!** Book 119.

[_] 40-120 — "Do People Go to Heaven when they Die?" (The Unbelievable Truth about Life and Death!) **By The Good Pastor of Uncommon Sense!** Book 120.

[_] 40-121 — "The Hopeless Church of Little Faith!" (The Unholy Church of Graceful Sinners, who are Mostly just Liars and Hypocrites!) **By The Good Pastor of Uncommon Sense!** Book 121.

{NOTE: That List of Available Books will be Updated, Periodically, if we do not get Killed by some Thugs, who Work for those Lying Conniving Edomites!}